ECLECTIC EL

MᶜGUFFEY'S

FOURTH

ECLECTIC READER

REVISED EDITION

NEW WEST PRESS

PREFACE.

In revising the FOURTH READER, the aim has been—as it has with the other books of the Series—to preserve unimpaired all the essential characteristics of MᶜGUFFEY'S READERS. New articles have been substituted for old ones only where the advantage was manifest.

The book has been considerably enlarged, and has been liberally illustrated by the first artists of the country, as shown in the Table of Contents.

It can not be presumed that every pupil has at hand all the works of reference necessary for the proper preparation of each lesson; hence all the aids that seem requisite to this purpose have been given. Brief notices concerning the various authors represented have been inserted; the more difficult words have been defined, and their pronunciation has been indicated by diacritical marks; and short explanatory notes have been given wherever required for a full understanding of the text.

Especial acknowledgment is due to Messrs. Houghton, Osgood & Co. for their permission to make liberal selections from their copyright editions of many of the foremost American author whose works they publish.

Copyright © 2021   ISBN: Paperback: 978-1-64965-191-4   Hardcover: 978-1-64965-319-2

CONTENTS

INTRODUCTORY MATTER.

SELECTIONS IN PROSE AND POETRY.

CONTENTS

PUNCTUATION MARKS.

1. The **Hyphen** (-) is used between syllables and between the parts of a compound word; as, No-ble, col-o-ny, and text- book, easy-chair.

2. The **Comma** (,), the **Semicolon** (;), and the **Colon** (:) denote grammatical divisions.

NOTE—These marks do not indicate the comparative length of the pauses to be made where they occur.

3. The **Period** (.) is placed at the end of a sentence. It is also used after an abbreviation; as, God is love. Dr. Eben Goodwin.

4. The **Interrogation point** (?) denotes a question; as, Has he come? Who are you?

5. The **Exclamation point** (!) denotes strong feeling; as, Oh Absalom! my son! my son!

6. **Quotation marks** (" ") denote the words of another; as, God said, "Let there be light."

7. **The Apostrophe** (') denotes that a letter or letters are left out; as, O'er, for over; 't is, for it is.

It also denotes the possessive case; as, John's hat.

8. **The Curves** ( ) include what, if omitted, would not obscure the sense. The parenthesis, or words included by the curves, should be read in a low key, and with greater rapidity than the rest of the sentence.

9. **Brackets** [ ] include something intended to exemplify what goes before, or to supply some deficiency, or rectify some mistake.

10. **A Dash** (–) denotes a long or significant pause, or an abrupt change or transition in a sentence.

11. Marks of Ellipsis (***) indicate the omission of letters of a word, or words of a sentence; as, P * * * * e J**n, for Prince John; the ******* was hung, for the traitor was hung.

Sometimes a long line, or a succession of dots is used instead of stars; as, J—n A———s, for John Adams; the D..e W.....m, for the Duke William.

12. A **Brace** (}) is used to connect several lines or words together.

13. A **Diaeresis** (¨) is put over the latter of two vowels, to show that they belong to two distinct syllables; thus, coöperate.

14. A **Section** (§) is used to divide a discourse or chapter into parts.

15. An **Index** (☞) points out something that requires particular attention.

16. A **Paragraph** (¶) denotes a new subject. It is used in the common version of the Bible.

17. Certain marks(*,†, ‡, ‖, §) and sometimes figures and letters are used to refer to some remark in the margin.

18. A **Caret** (^) is used in writing, to show that some-thing is omitted; as,

      n   her
Maner. I love for her modesty and virtue.
     ^   ^

ARTICULATION.

ELEMENTARY SOUNDS.

Articulation is the utterance of the elementary sounds of a language, and of their combinations.

An **Elementary Sound** is a simple, distinct sound made by the organs of speech.

The Elementary Sounds of the English language are divided into *Vocals*, *Subvocals*, and *Aspirates*.

Vocals are those sounds which consist of pure tone only. They are the most prominent elements of speech. A diphthong is a union of two vocals, commencing with one and ending with the other.

Subvocals are those sounds in which the vocalized breath is more or less obstructed.

Aspirates consist of breath only, modified by the vocal organs.

VOCALS.

DIRECTIONS FOR ARTICULATION. 1. Let the mouth be open, and the teeth, tongue, and palate in their proper position. 2. Pronounce the word in the CHART forcibly, and with the falling inflection, several times in succession; then drop the subvocal or aspirate sounds which precede or follow the vocal, and repeat the vocals alone.

TABLE.

Long Vocals.

ā,	as	in	hāte.			ē,	as	in	ēve.
â,	"		hâre.			ẽ,	"		ẽrr.
ä,	"		fär.			ī,	"		pīne.
ȧ,	"		pȧss.			ō,	"		nō.
ạ,	"		fạll.			ū,	"		tūbe.

ōō, as in ꞓōōl

Short Vocals.

ă,	as	in	măt.			ŏ,	as	in	hŏt.
ĕ,	"		mĕt.			ŭ,	"		ŭs.
ĭ,	"		ĭt.			oo,	"		book.

REMARK.—In this table, the short sounds, except u, are nearly or quite the same, in quality, as certain of the long sounds. The difference consists chiefly in quantity. As a rule, the long vocals should be prolonged with a full, clear utterance; but the short vocals should be uttered sharply and almost explosively.

Diphthongs.

oi, oy, as in coin, boy. | ou, ow, as in noun, now.

SUBVOCALS AND ASPIRATES.

DIRECTIONS FOR ARTICULATION. Pronounce distinctly and forcibly, several times in succession, words in which these sounds occur as elements; then drop the other sounds, and repeat the subvocals and aspirates alone. Each subvocal in the first table should be practiced in connection with its cognate sound.

LET the class repeat the words and elements, at first in concert; then separately.

SELECT words ending with subvocal sounds for practice on subvocals; words beginning or ending with aspirate sounds, for practice on aspirates.

COGNATE SOUNDS.

Subvocals.	*Aspirates.*

b,	as	in	babe.	p,	as	in	rap.
d,	"		rod.	t,	"		at.
g,	"		fog.	k,	"		book.
j,	"		judge.	ch,	"		chat.
v,	"		live.	f,	"		file.
th,	"		them.	th,	"		myth.
z,	"		buzz.	s,	"		sink.
zh,	"		azure.	sh,	"		shine.
w,	"		win.	wh,	"		when.

REMARK.—These eighteen sounds make nine pairs of cognate sounds. In articulating the aspirates, the vocal organs are put in the position as required for the articulation of the corresponding subvocals; but the breath is expelled with some force, without the utterance of any vocal sound. Let the pupil verify this by experiment, and then practice on these cognates.

THE following sounds are not cognates.

SUBVOCALS.

l,	as	in	mill.	ng,		as in sing, think.
m,	"		him.	r, (rough)	"	rule.
n,	"		tin.	r, (smooth)	"	car.

y as in yet.

ASPIRATE.

h as in hat.

SUBSTITUTES.

Substitutes are characters used to represent sounds ordinarily represented by other characters. The following table indicates nearly every form of substitution used in the language: a few exceptional cases only are omitted

TABLE OF SUBSTITUTES.

a	for	ĕ,	as in	any.	ọ	for	ōō,	as in	tọ.
ạ	"	ŏ,	"	whạt.	ọ	"	oo,	"	wọuld.
c	"	z,	"	suffīce.	ȯ	"	ŭ,	"	sȯn.
ç	"	s,	"	çīte.	ph	"	v,	"	Stēphen.
€	"	k,	"	€ăp.	ph	"	f,	"	sӯlph.
€h	"	k,	"	ā€he.	q	"	k,	"	lĭquor.
çh	"	sh,	"	maçhïne.	qu	"	kw,	"	quōte.
d	"	j,	"	sōldier.	s	"	sh,	"	sure.
e	"	ĭ,	"	England.	ṣ	"	zh,	"	rāṣūre.
ê	"	â,	"	thêre.	ṣ	"	z,	"	rōṣe.
ẹ	"	ā,	"	fẹint.	u	"	ĕ,	"	bury.
ee	"	ĭ,	"	been.	u	"	ĭ,	"	busy.
f	"	v,	"	ŏf.	û	"	ē,	"	ûrge.
ġ	"	j,	"	€āġe.	ụ	"	ōō,	"	rụde.
gh	"	f,	"	läugh.	ụ	"	oo,	"	pụll.
gh	"	k,	"	lŏugh.	x	"	ks,	"	wăx.
ï	"	ē,	"	polïçe.	x	"	ksh,	"	nŏxious.
ī	"	ē,	"	thīrst.	x	"	z,	"	Xĕrxes.
i	"	y,	"	fĭlial.	x	"	gz,	"	exămĭne.
n	"	ng,	"	rĭnk.	y	"	ē,	"	mӯrrh.
o	"	ē,	"	work.	y	"	ī,	"	mӯ.
o	"	ĭ,	"	women.	y	"	ĭ,	"	hӯmn.
ô	"	ạ,	"	fôrm.	z	"	s,	"	quạrtz.

VOCALS.

Let the teacher utter each word, and then its vocal sound, and let the pupil imitate *closely* and *carefully*, thus:

Māte, ā; Rāte, ā: Măn, ă: Fär, ä: etc.

ā.—Māte, rāin, sāy, thẹy, fẹint, gāuge, breāk, vẹin, gāol.

ă.—Măn, păn, tăn, shăll, lămp, băck, măt, stănd.

ä.—Fär, härd, äh, äunt, heärt, guärd, psälm.

ạ.—Bạll, tạlk, pạuse, sạw, broạd, stôrm, nạught, bôught.

ạ.—Wạs, whạt, wạsh, swạp, nŏd, blŏt, knŏwledge.

ē.—Mē, trēe, sēa, kēy, fiēld, cēiling, pēople, polïçe.

ĕ.—Mĕt, brĕad, said (sĕd), says (sĕz), friĕnd, hĕifer, lĕopard, guĕss, any (ĕn′y), bury (bĕr′ry).

ē.—Hēr, clērk, ēarn, wēre, dūrst, fīrst, work, mȳrrh.

ī.—Pīne, sīgn, līe, tȳpe, sleīght, buȳ, guīde, aīsle, choīr.

ĭ.—Pĭn, fountaĭn, been (bĭn), busy (bĭz′y), surfeĭt, sĭeve, hȳmn, buĭld, mȳth.

ī.—Sīr, bīrd, gīrl, bīrch, mīrth, bīrth.

ō.—Nō, dōōr, lōam, hōe, sōul, snōw, sew (sō), yeōmen, bureau (bu′rō), hautboy (hō′boy).

ŏ.—Nŏt, blŏt, chŏp, thrŏb, bŏther, bŏdy, wạn.

ô.—Nôr, bôrn, stôrm, côrk, fôrk, smạll, stạll.

ọ.—Wọlf, wọman, bụshel, wọuld, shọuld, pụll

ọ.—Mọve, whọ, tọmb, grọup, sọup, shọe, dọ, lọse.

ȯ.—Lȯve, sȯn, flȯod, frȯnt, shȯve, tȯuch, dȯes, tȯngue.

ŏŏ.—Wŏŏl, bŏŏk, cŏŏk, rŏŏk, gŏŏdly.

ōō.—Fōōd, trōōp, tōōth, gōōse, spōōn, nōōn.

ū.—Use, abūse, beāūty, feūd, view, adieū.

ŭ.—Rŭb, sŭm, sŭn, sŭch, mŭch, tŭck, lŭck, trŏŭble.

û.—Fûr, cûrl, hûrt, bûrn, tûrn, spûrn.

ụ.—Fụll, bụll, pụsh, bụsh.

oi, oy.–Oil, point, voice, noise, boiler, boy, joy, alloy.

ou, ow.–Our, sour, cloud, owl, now, bow, couch.

SUBVOCALS.

Let the *sound* of each letter be given, and not its name. After articulating the *sounds*, each word should be pronounced distinctly.

b.—Be, by, boy, bib, sob, bite, bone, band, bubble.

d.—Deed, did, dab, bid, bud, dead, door, indeed.

g.—Go, gag, gig, bag, beg, fog, fig, girl, rag, log.

j.—Jay, joy, jig, gill, job, judge, ginger, soldier.

l.—Lad, led, dell, mill, line, lily, folly.

m—Me, my, mad, mug, him, aim, blame.

n.—No, now, nab, nod, man, sun, none, noun.

r. (rough)—Rear, red, rough, riot, ripe, rude, ragged.

r. (smooth)—Form, farm, worn, for, ear, manner.

v.—Van, vine, vale, vivid, stove, of, Stephen.
w.—We, woe, web, wed, wig, wag, wood, will, wonder.
y.—Ye, yam, yon, yes, yarn, yoke, yawn, filial.
z.—Zag, rose, rise, zone, lives, stars, suffice.
zh.—Azure, osier, usual, measure, rouge (roozh).
th.—Thee, thy, them, blithe, beneath, those.
ng.—Bang, fang, gang, bring, sing, fling.

ASPIRATES.

f.—Fib, fob, buff, beef, if, off, life, phrase, laugh.
h.—Ha, he, hub, had, how, hill, home, hire, horse.
k.—Kill, bake, cat, cow, come, chord, black.
p.—Pop, pig, lip, map, pipe, pope, apple, path, pile.
s.—Sad, fuss, miss, cent, cease, sick, sound, sincere.
t.—Hat, mat, toe, totter, tint, time, sleet, taught.
sh.—Dash, shad, rush, sure, ocean, notion, passion, chaise.
ch.—Chin, chop, chat, rich, much, church, bastion.
th.—Thin, hath, think, teeth, truth, breath, pith.

SUBVOCALS COMBINED.

br.—Bred, brag, brow, brim, brush, breed, brown.
bz, bst.—Fibs, fib'st, robs, rob'st, rubs, rub'st.
bd, bdst.—Fibbed, fib'd'st, sobbed, sob'd'st, robbed, rob'd'st.
bl.—Blab, blow, bluff, bliss, stable, babble, gobble.
blz, blst.—Fables, fabl'st, nibbles, nibbl'st.
bld, bldst.—Fabled, fabl'd'st, nibbled, nibbl'd'st.

dr.—Drab, drip, drop, drag drum, dress, drink.
dz, dst.—Rids, rid'st, adds, add'st, sheds, shed'st.
dl.—Addle, paddle, fiddle, riddle, needle, idle, ladle.
dlz, dlst.—Addles, addl'st, fiddles, fiddl'st.
dld.—Addled, fiddled, huddled, idled, ladled.

fr.—Fret, frog, from, fry, fresh, frame, free.
fs, fst.—Cuffs, cuff'st, stuffs, stuff'st, doffs, doff'st.
ft.—Lift, waft, drift, graft, soft, theft, craft, shaft.
fts, ftst.—Lifts, lift'st, wafts, waft'st, sifts, sift'st.
fl.—Baffle, raffle, shuffle, muffle, rifle, trifle, whiffle.
fls, flst.—Baffles, baffl'st, shuffles, shuffl'st, rifles, rifl'st.
fld, fldst.—Baffled, baffl'd'st, shuffled, shuffl'd'st.

gr.—Grab, grim, grip, grate, grant, grass, green.
gz, gst.—Begs, beg'st, digs, dig'st, gags, gag'st.
gd, gdst.—Begged, begg'd'st, digged, digg'd'st.
gl.—Higgle, joggle, straggle, glib, glow, glaze.
glz, glst.—Higgles, higgl'st, juggles, juggl'st.
gld, gldst.—Higgled, higgl'd'st, joggled, joggl'd'st.

jd.—Caged, hedged, bridged, lodged, judged, waged.
kr.—Cram, crag, crash, crop, cry, creel, crone, crown.
kw, (qu).—Quell, quick, quite, quote, quake, queen.
ks, kst, (x).—Kicks, kick'st, mix, mixed, box, boxed.
kt, kts.—Act, acts, fact, facts, tact, tacts, sect, sects.
kl.—Clad, clip, clown, clean, close, cackle, pickle.
klz, klst.—Cackles, cackl'st, buckles, buckl'st.
kld, kldst.—Cackled, cackl'd'st, buckled, buckl'd'st.

lf.—Elf, Ralph, shelf, gulf, sylph, wolf.
ld.—Hold, mold, bold, cold, wild, mild, field, yield.
ldz, ldst.—Holds, hold'st, gilds, gild'st, yields, yield'st.
lz, lst.—Fills, fill'st, pulls, pull'st, drills, drill'st.
lt, lts.—Melt, melts, tilt, tilts, salt, salts, bolt, bolts.
mz, mst.—Names, nam'st, hems, hem'st, dims, dim'st.
md, mdst.—Named, nam'd'st, dimmed, dimm'd'st.

nd.—And, lend, band, blonde, fund, bound, round, sound.
ndz, ndst.—Lends, lend'st, hands, hand'st.
ndl.—Handle, kindle, fondle, trundle, brindle.
ndlz, ndlst.—Handles, halldl'st, kindles, kindl'st.
ndld, ndldst.—Handled, handl'd'st, kindled, kindl'd'st.

nks, nkst.—Banks, hank'st, sinks, sink'st.
nkd.—Banked, clank'd, winked, thank'd, flank'd.

nz, nst.—Wins, win'st, tans, tan'st, runs run'st.
nt, nts.—Hint, hints, cent, cents, want, wants.
nch, nchd.—Pinch, pinch'd, blanch, blanch'd.
ngz, ngd.—Hangs, hang'd, rings, ring'd.
nj, njd.—Range, ranged, hinge, hinged.
pr.—Prat, prim, print, prone, prune, pry, prank.

pl.—Plant, plod, plum, plus, apple, cripple.
ps, pst.—Nips, nip'st, taps, tap'st, mops, mop'st.
pt, pts.—Adopt, adopts, adept, adepts, crypt, crypts.

rj, rjd.—Merge, merged, charge, charged, urge, urged.
rd.—Card, cord, curd, herd, ford, ward, bird.
rdz, rdst.—Cards, card'st, herds, herd'st, cords, cord'st.
rk.—Bark, jerk, dirk, cork, lurk, work.
rks, rkst.—Barks, bark'st, lurks, lurk'st.
rl.—Marl, curl, whirl, pearl, whorl, snarl.
rlz, rlst.—Curls, curl'st, whirls, whirl'st, twirls, twirl'st.
rld, rldst.— Curled, curl'd'st, whirled, whirl'd'st, snarled,
    snarl'd'st.

rm.—Arm, term, form, warm, storm, worm, sperm.
rmz, rmst.—Arms, arm'st, fbrms, form'st. rmd,
rmdst.—Armed, arm'd'st, formed, form'd'st.
rn.—Barn, warn, scorn, worn, earn, turn.
rnz, rnst.—Turns, turn'st, scorns, scorn'st.
rnd, rndst.—Turned, turn'd'st, scorned, scorn'd'st.
rt.—Dart, heart, pert, sort, girt, dirt, hurt.
rts, rtst.—Darts, dart'st, girts, girt'st, hurts, hurt'st.
rch, rchd.—Arch, arched, perch, perched.

sk.—Ask, scab, skip, risk, skum, bask, husk.
sks.—Asks, tasks. risks, whisks, husks.
skd, skst.—Asked, ask'st, risked, risk'st, husked, husk'st. sp,
sps.—Gasp, gasps, rasp, rasps, crisp, crisps.

spd.—Gasped, lisped, crisped, wisped, cusped.
st, sts.—Mast, masts, nest, nests, fist, fists.
sw.—Swim, swell, swill, swan, sweet, swing, swam.
str.—Strap, strip, strop, stress, strut, strife, strew.

tl.—Rattle, nettle, whittle, bottle, hurtle, scuttle.
tlz, tlst.—Rattles, rattl'st, nettles, nettl'st.
tld, tldst.—Rattled, rattl'd'st, settled, settl'd'st.
ts, tst.—Bat, bat'st, bets, bet'st, pits, pit'st, dots, dot'st.
tw.—Twin, twirl, twice, tweed, twist, twelve, twain.
tr.—Trap, trip, trot, tress, truss, trash, try, truce, trice.
vz, vst.—Gives, giv'st, loves, lov'st, saves, sav'st.

zm, zmz.—Chasm, chasms, prism, prisms.
zl.—Dazzle, frizzle, nozzle, puzzle.
zlz, zld.—Dazzles, dazzled, frizzles, frizzled.
sht.—Dashed, meshed, dished, rushed, washed.
shr.—Shrank, shred, shrill, shrunk, shrine, shroud, shrew.
thd.—Bathed, sheathed, soothed, smoothed, wreathed.
thz, thzt.—Bathes, Bath'st, sheathes, sheath'st.
ngz, ngst.—Hangs, hang'st, brings, bring'st.

ngd, ngdst.—Hanged, hang'd'st., stringed, string'd'st.
nks, nkst.—Thanks, thank'st, thinks, think'st.
nkd, nkdst.—Thanked, thank'd'st, kinked, kink'd'st.
dth, dths.—Width, widths, breadth, breadths.
kld, kldst.—Circled, circl'd'st, darkle, darkl'd'st.
kl, klz.—Circle, circles, cycle, cycles.
lj, ljd.—Bilge, bilged, bulge, bulged, indulge, indulged.
lb, lbz.—Alb, albs, bulb, bulbs.
lk, lks, lkst, lkdst.—Milk, milks, milk'st, milk'd'st.

lm, lmz.—Elm, elms, whelm, whelms, film, films.
lp, lpd, lpst, lpdst.—Help, helped, help'st, help'd'st.
lv, lvz, lvd.—Valve, valves, valved, delve, delves, delved.
lch, lchd.—Belch, belched, filch, filched, gulch, gulched.
lth, lths —Health, healths, tilth, tilth

mf, mfs.—Nymph, nymphs, triumph, triumphs.

gth, gths.—Length, lengths, strength, strengths.

rb, rbz, rbd, rbst, rbdst.—Curb, curbs, curbed, curb'st, curb'd'st.

rf, rfs, rfst, rfdst.—Dwarf, dwarfs, dwarf'st, dwarf'd'st.

rv, rvz, rvst, rvd, rvdst.—Curve, curves, curv'st, curved, curv'd'st.

rth, rths.—Birth, births, girth, girths, hearth, hearths.

rp, rps, rpd, rpst, rpdst.—Harp, harps, harped, harp'st, harp'd'st.

rs, rst.—Nurse, nursed, verse, versed, course, coursed.

thr.—Thrash, thresh, thrift, throb, thrush, thrust, throng, three, thrive, thrice, throat, throne, throve, thrill, thrum.

thw.—Thwack, thwart.

———

EXERCISES IN ARTICULATION.

Errors to be Corrected.

To Teachers.—In the following exercises, the more common errors in articulation and pronunciation are denoted. The letters in *italics* are not *silent* letters, but are thus marked to point them out as the representatives of sounds which are apt to be defectively articulated, omitted, or incorrectly sounded.

A

INCORRECT.		CORRECT.	INCORRECT.		CORRECT.
Fa-t'l	*for*	fa-t*a*l	Sep-er-ate	*for*	sep-*a*-rate
reel	"	re-*a*l	temp-per-*u*nce	"	tem-per-*a*nce
ras-c*u*l	"	ras-c*a*l	up-pear	"	ap-pear
crit-ic-*u*l	"	crit-ic-*a*l	tem-per-*i*t	"	tem-per-*a*te
test'ment	"	tes-t*a*-ment	mod-er-*i*t	"	med-er-*a*te
firm'ment	"	fir-m*a*-ment	in-ti-m*i*t	"	int-ti-m*a*te

E

INCORRECT.		CORRECT.		INCORRECT.		CORRECT.
Ev'ry	*for*	ev-er-y.		sev'ral	*for*	sev-er-al.
b'lief	"	be-lief.		prov-i-dunce	"	prov-i-dence.
pr'vail	"	pre-vail.		ev-i-dunce	"	ev-i-dence.
r'tain	"	re-tain.		si-lunt	"	si-lent.
trav'ler	"	trav-el-er.		mon-u-munt	"	mon-u-ment.
flut'ring	"	flut-ter-ing.		con-ti-nunt	"	con-ti-nent.
tel'scope	"	tel-e-scope		con-fi-dunt	"	con-fi-dent.

I

INCORRECT.		CORRECT.		INCORRECT.		CORRECT.
D'rect	*for*	di-rect.		rad'cal	*for*	rad-i-cal.
d'spose	"	dis-pose.		sal'vate	"	sal-i-vate.
van'ty	"	van-i-ty.		can'bal	"	can-ni-bal.
ven-t'late	"	ven-ti-late.		mount'n	"	mount-ain.
ju-b'lee	"	ju-bi-lee.		fount'n	"	fount-ain.
rid'cule	"	rid-i-cule.		vill'ny	"	vil-lain-y.

O

INCORRECT.		CORRECT.		INCORRECT.		CORRECT.
Des'late	*for*	des-o-late.		rhet-er-ic	*for*	rhet-o-ric.
hist'ry	"	his-to-ry.		in-ser-lent	"	in-so-lent.
mem'ry	"	mem-o-ry..		croc-ud-ile	"	croc-o-dile.
col'ny	"	col-o-ny.		com-prum-ise	"	com-pro-mise.
ag'ny	"	ag-o-ny.		anch-ur-ite	"	anch-o-rite.
balc'ny	"	bal-co-ny.		cor-per-al	"	cor-po-ral.
ob-s'lete	"	ob-so-lete.		ob-luq-quy	"	ob-lo-quy.
wil-ler	"	wil-low.		or-ther-dox	"	or-tho-dox.
wid-der	"	wid-ow.		cun-di-tion	"	con-di-tion.
pil-ler	"	pil-low.		pus-i-tion	"	po-si-tion.
mead-er	"	mead-ow.		tug-eth-er	"	to-geth-er.
fel-ler	"	fel-low.		put-a-ter	"	po-ta-to.
win-der	"	win-dow		tub-ac-cur	"	to-bac-co.

U

THE most common mistake in the sound of u occurs in words of the following kind: as, crea-t*er* or crea-*choor*, for crea-*u*re; na-t*er* or na- *choor* for na-t-*ure*, etc.

INCORRECT.		CORRECT.	PRONOUNCED.
Lec´-ter or lec´-choor	*for*	lec´-ture	lĕ€t´-yur.
fea´-ter or fea´-choor	"	fea´-ture	fēat´-yur.
mois´-ter or mois´-choor	"	mois´-ture	moist´-yur.
ver´-der or ver´-jer	"	ver-dure	vĕrd´-yur.
mix´-ter or mix´-cher	"	mix´-ture	mĭxt´-yur.
rup´ter or rup´-cher	"	rup´-ture	rŭpt´-yur.
sculp´-ter or sculp´-cher	"	sculp´-ture	s€ŭlptŭ´-yur.
ges´-ter or ges´cher	"	ges´-ture	ġĕst´-yur.
struc´-ter or struc´-cher	"	struc´-ture	strŭ€t´-yur.
stric´-ter or stric´-choor	"	stric´-ture	strĭ€t´-yur.
ves´-ter or ves´-cher	"	ves´-ture	vĕst´-yur.
tex´-ter or tex´-cher	"	tex´-ture	tĕxt´-yur.
fix´-ter or fix´-cher	"	fix´-ture	fĭxt´-yur.
vul´-ter or vul´-cher	"	vul´-ture	vŭlt´-yur.
for´-ten or for´-choon	"	for´-tune	fôrt´-yune.
stat´-er or sta´-choor	"	stat´-ure	stăt´-yur.
stat´-ew or stat´-choo	"	stat´ue	stăt´-yu.
stat´-ewt or sta´-choot	"	stat´-ute	stăt´-yute.
ed´-di-cate or ed´-ju-cate	"	ed´-u-cate	ĕd´-yu-cate.

H

In order to accustom the learner to sound H properly, let him pronounce certain words *without* and then *with* it: as aft, *h*aft; ail, *h*ail, etc. The *H* should be clearly sounded.

Aft	*H*aft.	Edge	*H*edge.
Ail	*H*ail.	Eel.	*H*eel.
Air	*H*air.	Ell	*H*ell.
All	*H*all.	Elm	*H*elm.
Ark	*H*ark.	Eye	*H*igh.
Arm	*H*arm.	Ill	*H*ill.
Art	*H*art.	It	*H*it.
Ash	*H*ash.	Old	*H*old.
At	*H*at.	Yew	*H*ew.

D *Final.*

INCORRECT.		CORRECT.	INCORRECT.		CORRECT.
An	*for*	and.	frien	*for*	friend.
lan	"	land.	soun	"	sound.
mine	"	mind.	groun	"	ground.
boun	"	bound.	fiel	"	field.

K *Final.*

INCORRECT.		CORRECT.	INCORRECT.		CORRECT.
Fris	*for*	frisk.	dus	*for*	dusk.
des	"	desk.	mos	"	mosque.
tas	"	task.	tus	"	tusk.
ris	"	risk.	hus	"	husk.

K *for* Ng.

INCORRECT.		CORRECT.	INCORRECT.		CORRECT.
Morn-in	*for*	morn-ing.	shav-in	*for*	shav-ing.
run-nin	"	run-ning.	hid-in	"	hid-ing.
talk-in	"	talk-ing.	see-in	"	see-ing.
walk-in	"	walk-ing.	lov-in	"	lov-ing.
drink-in	"	drink-ing.	fight-in	"	fight-ing.
slid-in	"	slid-ing.	laugh-in	"	laugh-ing.

R

Sound the R *clearly* and *forcibly*. When it *precedes* a vowel, give it a slight trill.

Rule.	ruin.	rat.	rug.	reck.	rate.
reed.	rill.	rub.	rig.	rim	rite
ride.	rise.	red.	rag.	rick.	rote.
run.	reek.	rib.	rob.	rip.	ruse.
roar.	roam.	rack.	rid.	ripe.	rouse.

Arch.	farm.	lark.	far.	snare.	for.
march.	barm.	bark.	bar.	spare.	war.
larch.	charm.	mark.	hair.	sure.	corn.
starch.	dark.	are.	stair.	lure.	born.
arm.	spark.	star.	care.	pure.	horn.

T *Final.*

INCORRECT.		CORRECT.	INCORRECT.		CORRECT.
Eas	*for*	east.	wep	*for*	wept.
moce	"	most.	ob-jec	"	ob-ject.
los	"	lost.	per-fec	"	per-fect.
nes	"	nest.	dear-es	"	dear-est.
gues	"	guest.	high-es	"	high-est.

TS *Final.*

INCORRECT.		CORRECT.	INCORRECT.		CORRECT.
Hoce	*for*	hosts.	sec's	*for*	sects.
tes	"	tests.	bus	"	busts.
lif's	"	lifts.	cense	"	cents.
tuff's	"	tufts.	ob-jec's	"	ob-jects.
ac's	"	acts.	re-spec's	"	re-spects.

W *for* Wh.

INCORRECT.		CORRECT.	INCORRECT.		CORRECT.
Wale	*for*	Whale.	Wet	*for*	Whet.
Weal	"	Wheel.	Wine	"	Whine.
Wen	"	When.	Wip	"	Whip.

SENTENCES FOR PRACTICE.

Sentences like the following may be read with great advantage, for the purpose of acquiring distinctness and precision in articulation.

This *act*, more than all other *acts*, laid the ax at the root of the evil. It is *false* to say he had no other *faults*.

The *hosts* still stand in strangest plight. That last still night. That lasts *till* night. On either side *an* ocean exists. On neither side a *notion* exists. Among the rugged rocks the restless ranger ran. I said *pop-u-lar*, not pop'lar. I said *pre-vail*, not pr'vail. I said *be-hold*, not b'hold.

Think'st thou so meanly of my *Phocion? Henceforth* look to your *hearths*. Canst thou *minister* to a *mind* diseased? A thousand *shrieks* for hopeless mercy call.

ACCENT.

Accent, marked thus ('), is an increased force of voice upon some one syllable of a word; as,

Col'o-ny, bot'a-ny; re-mem'ber, im-por'tant; rec-ol-lect', rep-re-sent'. In the words *col'o-ny* and *bot'a-ny*, the *first* syllable is accented. In the words *re‿mem'ber* and *im-por'tant*, the second syllable is accented. In the words *rec-ol-lect'* and *rep-re‿sent'*, the *third* syllable is accented.

INFLECTION.

Inflection is an upward or downward slide of the voice.

The **Rising Inflection**, sometimes marked thus ('), is an upward slide of the voice.

EXAMPLES.

Has he come'? To be read thus: . . Has he come?
Has he gone'? . . . . Has he gone?
Are you sick'? . . . . . . Are you sick?
Will you go'? . . . . Will you go?
Are they here'? . . . . . . Are they here?

The **Falling Inflection**, marked thus (`) is a *downward* slide of the voice.

EXAMPLES.

They are here`. To be read thus: . . They are here.
He has gone`. . . . . He has gone.
He has come`. . . . . He has come.
I will go`. . . . . I will go.
I am well`. . . . . I am well.

Let the pupil practice these examples until he is perfectly familiar with the rising and falling inflections.

Are you sick, or well?   Will you go, or stay?

Did he ride, or walk?   Is it black, or white?

Is he rich, or poor?   Are they old, or young?

Did you say cap, or cat?   I said cat, not cap.

Did you say am, or ham?   I said ham, not am.

Is the dog white´, or black`? The dog is black`, not white´. Did you say and´, or hand`? I said and`, not hand´. Is the tree large´, or small`? The tree is small`, not large´. Are the apples sweet´, or sour`? The apples are sour` not sweet´. Is the tide high´, or low`? The tide is high´, not low`. Did you say play´, or pray`? I said pray`, not play´.

I. PERSEVERANCE.

1. "WILL you give my kite a lift?" said my little nephew to his sister, after trying in vain to make it fly by dragging it along the ground. Lucy very kindly took it up and threw it into the air, but, her brother neglecting to run off at the same moment, the kite fell down again.

2. "Ah! now, how awkward you are!" said the little fellow. "It was your fault entirely," answered his sister. "Try again, children," said I.

3. Lucy once more took up the kite. But now John was in too great a hurry; he ran off so suddenly that he twitched the kite out of her hand, and it fell flat as before. "Well, who is to blame now?" asked Lucy. "Try again," said I.

4. They did, and with more care; but a side wind coming suddenly, as Lucy let go the kite, it was blown against some shrubs, and the tail became entangled in a moment, leaving the poor kite hanging with its head downward.

5. "There, there!" exclaimed John, "that comes of your throwing it all to one side." "As if I could make the wind blow straight," said Lucy. In the meantime, I went to the kite's assistance; and having disengaged the long tail, I rolled it up, saying, "Come, children, there are too many trees here; let us find a more open space, and then try again."

6. We presently found a nice grass-plot, at one side of which I took my stand; and all things being prepared, I tossed the kite up just as little John ran off. It rose with all the dignity of a balloon, and promised a lofty flight; but John, delighted to find it pulling so hard at the string, stopped short to look upward and admire. The string slackened, the kite wavered, and, the wind not being very favorable, down came the kite to the grass. "O John, you should not have stopped," said I. "However, try again."

7. "I won't try any more," replied he, rather sullenly. "It is of no use, you see. The kite won't fly, and I don't want to be plagued with it any longer." "Oh, fie, my little man! would you give up the sport,

after all the pains we have taken both to make and to fly the kite? A few disappointments ought not to discourage us. Come, I have wound up your string, and now try again."

8. And he did try, and succeeded, for the kite was carried upward on the breeze as lightly as a feather; and when the string was all out, John stood in great delight, holding fast the stick and gazing on the kite, which now seemed like a little white speck in the blue sky. "Look, look, aunt, how high it flies! and it pulls like a team of horses, so that I can hardly hold it. I wish I had a mile of string: I am sure it would go to the end of it."

9. After enjoying the sight as long as he pleased, little John proceeded to roll up the string slowly; and when the kite fell, he took it up with great glee, saying that it was not at all hurt, and that it had behaved very well. "Shall we come out to-morrow, aunt, after lessons, and try again?"

10. "I have no objection, my dear, if the weather is fine. And now, as we walk home, tell me what you have learned from your morning's sport." "I have learned to fly my kite properly." "You may thank aunt for it, brother," said Lucy, "for you would have given it up long ago, if she had not persuaded you to try again."

11. "Yes, dear children, I wish to teach you the value of perseverance, even when nothing more depends upon it than the flying of a kite. Whenever you fail in your attempts to do any good thing, let your motto be,—try again."

DEFINITIONS.—In defining words, that meaning is given which is appropriate to them in the connection in which they are used.

4. En-tăn′ḡled, *twisted in, disordered.* 5. As-sĭst′-ançe, *help, aid.* Dĭs-en-ḡāḡed′, *cleared, set free.* 6. Grȧss′-plŏt, *a space covered with grass.* Dĭg′ni-ty, *majestic manner.* 7. Dĭs-ap-point′ments, *fail-ures or defeats of expectation.* Dĭs-coŭr′aġe, *take away courage.* 9. Glee, *joy* 11. Pĕr-se-vēr′ançe, *continuance in anything once begun.* Mŏt′to, *a short sentence or a word full of meaning.*

EXERCISES—What is the subject of this lesson? Why was John discouraged in his attempts to fly his kite? What did his, aunt say to him? What may we learn from this? What should be our motto if we expect to be successful?

II. TRY, TRY AGAIN.

1. 'T is a lesson you should heed,
      Try, try again;
  If at first you don't succeed,
      Try, try again;
  Then your courage should appear,
  For, if you will persevere,
  You will conquer, never fear;
      Try, try again.

2. Once or twice though you should fail,
      Try, try again;
  If you would at last prevail,
      Try, try again;
  If we strive, 'tis no disgrace
  Though we do not win the race;
  What should you do in the case?
      Try, try again.

3. If you find your task is hard,
      Try, try again;

Time will bring you your reward,
　　Try, try again.
All that other folks can do,
Why, with patience, should not you?
Only keep this rule in view:
　　Try, try again

DEFINITIONS.—1. Coŭr′aġe, *resolution*. Cŏn′quer, *gain the*
victory. 2. Pre-vāil′, *overcome*. Dis-ḡrāçe′, *shame*. Wĭn, *gain, ob-*
tain. 3. Re-wạrd′, *anything given in return for good or bad con-*
duct. Pā′-tiençe, *constany in labor*.

EXERCISES.—What does the mark before "'T is" mean?
What is it called? What point is used after the word "case" in the
second verse? Why?

III. WHY THE SEA IS SALT.

A FAIRY TALE.

Mary Howitt was born in 1804, at Coleford, England. She wrote many
charming stories for children in prose and verse, and also translated many
from Swedish, Danish, and German authors. This story is arranged from
one in a collection named "Peter Drake's Dream, and Other Stories." She
died in 1888.

1. There were, in very ancient times, two brothers,
one of whom was rich, and the other poor. Christmas
was approaching, but the poor man had nothing in the
house for a Christmas dinner; so he went to his
brother and asked him for a trifling gift.

2. The rich man was ill-natured, and when he heard
his brother's request he looked very surly. But as
Christmas is a time when even the worst people give
gifts, he took a fine ham down from the chimney,
where it was hanging to smoke, threw it at his brother,
and bade him begone and never to let him see his face
again.

3. The poor man thanked his brother for the ham, put it under his arm, and went his way. He had to pass through a great forest on his way home. When he had reached the thickest part of it, he saw an old man, with a long, white beard, hewing timber. "Good evening," said he to him.

4. "Good evening," returned the old man, raising himself up from his work, and looking at him. "That is a fine ham you are carrying." On this, the poor man told him all about it.

5. "It is lucky for you," said the old man, "that you have met with me. If you will take that ham into the land of the dwarfs, the entrance to which lies just under the roots of this tree, you can make a capital bargain with it; for the dwarfs are very fond of ham, and rarely get any. But mind what I say: you must not sell it for money, but demand for it the 'old hand mill which stands behind the door.' When you come back, I'll show you how to use it."

6. The poor man thanked his new friend, who showed him the door under a stone below the roots of the tree, and by this door he entered into the land of the dwarfs. No sooner had he set his foot in it, than the dwarfs swarmed about him, attracted by the smell of the ham. They offered him queer, old-fashioned money and gold and silver ore for it; but he refused all their tempting offers, and said that he would sell it only for the old hand mill behind the door.

7. At this, the dwarfs held up their little old hands, and looked quite perplexed. "We can not make a bargain, it seems," said the poor man, "so I'll bid you all a good day."

8. The fragrance of the ham had by this time reached the remote parts of dwarf land. The dwarfs

came flocking around in little troops, leaving their work of digging out precious ores, eager for the ham.

9. "Let him have the old mill," said some of the new-comers; "it is quite out of order, and he don't know how to use it. Let him have it, and we will have the ham."

10. So the bargain was made. The poor man took the old hand mill, which was a little thing not half so large as the ham, and went back to the woods. Here the old man showed him how to use it. All this had taken up a great deal of time, and it was midnight before he reached home.

11. "Where in the world have you been?" said his wife. "Here I have been waiting and waiting, and we have no wood to make a fire, nor anything to put into the porridge pot for our Christmas supper."

12. The house was dark and cold; but the poor man bade his wife wait and see what would happen. He placed the little hand mill on the table, and began to turn the crank. First, out there came some grand, lighted wax candles, and a fire on the hearth, and a por-ridge pot boiling over it, because in his mind he said they should come first. Then he ground out a table-cloth, and dishes, and spoons, and knives and forks.

13. He was himself astonished at his good luck, as you may believe; and his wife was almost beside herself with joy and astonishment. Well, they had a capital supper; and after it was eaten, they ground out of the mill every possible thing to make their house and themselves warm and comfortable. So they had a merry Christmas eve and morning.

DEFINITIONS.—1. Trī'-fling, *of small value*. 5. Hănd'-mĭll, *a mill turned by hand*. 6. At-trăet'ed, *drawn to, allured*. 7. Per-plĕxed', *puzzled*. 8. Frā'ğrançe, *sweetness of smell*.

IV. WHY THE SEA IS SALT.

(CONCLUDED.)

1. When the people went by the house to church, the next day, they could hardly believe their eyes. There was glass in the windows instead of a wooden shutter, and the poor man and his wife, dressed in nice new clothes, were seen devoutly kneeling in the church.

2. "There is something very strange in all this," said everyone. "Something very strange indeed," said the rich man, when three days afterwards he received an invitation from his once poor brother to a grand feast. And what a feast it was! The table was covered with a cloth as white as snow, and the dishes were all of silver or gold. The rich man could not, in his great house, and with all his wealth, set out such a table.

3. "Where did you get all these things?" exclaimed he. His brother told him all about the bargain he had made with the dwarfs, and putting the mill on the table, ground out boots and shoes, coats and cloaks, stockings, gowns, and blankets, and bade his wife give them to the poor people that had gathered about the house to get a sight of the grand feast the poor brother had made for the rich one.

4. The rich man, was very envious of his brother's good fortune, and wanted to borrow the mill, intending—for he was not an honest man—never to return it again. His brother would not lend it, for the old man with the white beard had told him never to sell or lend it to anyone.

5. Some years went on, and, at last, the possessor of the mill built himself a grand castle on a rock by

the sea, facing the west. Its windows, reflecting the golden sunset, could be seen far out from the shore. It became a noted landmark for sailors. Strangers from foreign parts often came to see this castle and the wonderful mill of which the most extraordinary tales were told.

6. At length, a great foreign merchant came, and when he had seen the mill, inquired whether it would grind salt. Being told that it would, he wanted to buy it; for he traded in salt, and thought that if he owned it he could supply all his customers without taking long and dangerous voyages.

7. The man would not sell it, of course. He was so rich now that he did not want to use it for himself; but every Christmas he ground out food and clothes and coal for the poor, and nice presents for the little children. So he rejected all the offers of the rich merchant. The merchant, however, determined to have it; he bribed one of the man's servants to let him go into the castle at night, and he stole the mill and sailed away with it in triumph.

8. He had scarcely got out to sea, before he determined to set the mill to work. "Now, mill, grind salt," said he; "grind salt with all your might!—salt, salt, and nothing but salt!" The mill began to grind and the sailors to fill the sacks; but these were soon full, and in spite of all that could be done, it began to fill the ship.

9. The dishonest merchant was now very much frightened. What was to be done? The mill would not stop grinding; and at last the ship was overloaded, and down it went, making a great whirlpool where it sank. The ship soon went to pieces; but the mill stands on the bottom of the sea, and keeps grind-

ing out "salt, salt, nothing but salt!" That is the reason, say the peasants of Denmark and Norway, why the sea is salt.

DEFINITIONS.—1. De-vout´ly, *in a reverent manner.* 5. Re-flĕet´ing, *throwing back light, heat, etc., as a mirror.* Lănd´-märk, *an object on land serving as a guide to seamen.* Ex-traôr´di-na-ry, *wonderful.* 9. Whĭrl´-pōōl, *a gulf in which the water moves round in a circle.* Pĕaş´ants, *those belonging to the lowest class of tillers of the soil in Europe.*

EXERCISES.—What is a "fairy tale"? What fairy people are told about in this story? How did the poor man find the way to the land of the dwarfs? Do you think the old man would have told him if the poor man had not been so polite? How did the poor man treat his rich brother in return for his unkindness? How was the greed of the dishonest merchant punished? What is meant by "strangers from foreign parts"? Where are Denmark and Norway?

V. POPPING CORN.

1. One autumn night, when the wind was high,
   And the rain fell in heavy plashes,
   A little boy sat by the kitchen fire,
   A-popping corn in the ashes;
   And his sister, a curly-haired child of three,
   Sat looking on, just close to his knee.

2. Pop! pop! and the kernels, one by one,
   Came out of the embers flying;
   The boy held a long pine stick in his hand,
   And kept it busily plying;
   He stirred the corn and it snapped the more,
   And faster jumped to the clean-swept floor.

3. Part of the kernels flew one way,
   And a part hopped out the other;
   Some flew plump into the sister's lap,
   Some under the stool of the brother;
   The little girl gathered them into a heap,
   And called them a flock of milk-white sheep.

———

VI. SMILES.

1. Poor lame Jennie sat at her window, looking out upon the dismal, narrow street, with a look of pain and weariness on her face. "Oh, dear," she said with a sigh, "what a long day this is going to be," and she looked wishfully up the street.

2. Suddenly she leaned forward and pressed her pale face against the glass, as a rosy-checked boy came racing down the street, swinging his schoolbooks by the strap. Looking up to the window, he took off his hat and bowed with a bright, pleasant smile.

3. "What a nice boy he is," said Jennie to herself, as he ran out of sight. "I am so glad he goes by here on his way to school. When he smiles, it seems like having the sun shine. I wish everybody who goes by would look up and smile."

4. "Mamma," said George West, as he came from school, "I can't help thinking about that poor little girl I told you of the other day. She looks so tired. I took off my hat and bowed to her to-day. I wish I could do something for her,"

5. "Suppose you should carry her a handful of pretty flowers some time when you go to school," said Mrs. West. "I'll do that to-morrow morning," said George, "if I can find my way into that rickety old house."

6. The next morning, as Jennie sat leaning her head wearily against the window, watching the raindrops chasing one another down the glass, she spied George with a handful of beautiful flowers carefully picking his way across the street. He stopped in front of her window, and, smiling very pleasantly, said, "How shall I find the way to your room?"

7. Jennie pointed to an alley near by, where he turned in, and with some difficulty found his way to the dingy staircase. Opening the door to Jennie's gentle "Come in," he said, "I have brought you a handful of flowers to look at this rainy day."

8. "Are they for me?" exclaimed Jennie, clapping her hands in delight. "How kind you are," she cont-

tinued, as George laid them in her lap. "I have not had a flower since we live in the city."

9. "Did you use to live in the country?" asked George. "Oh, yes," answered Jennie, "we used to live in a beautiful cottage, and there were trees and flowers and green grass, and the air was so sweet."

10. "Well, what made you move here?" "Oh," said Jennie, softly, "papa died, and mamma was sick so long that the money was all gone. Then mamma had to sell the cottage, and she moved here to try to get work to do."

11. "Do you have to sit here all day?" asked George, glancing around the bare room and out into the dismal street. "Yes," said Jennie, "because I am lame; but I would not care for that, if I could only help mamma."

12. "I declare, it's too had!" said George, who dreaded nothing so much as being obliged to stay in the house. "Oh, no, it isn't," said Jennie, pleasantly; "mamma says maybe we should forget the Lord if we had everything we wanted, and He never forgets us, you know."

13. "Well, I must rush for school," said George, not knowing exactly what to say next; and he was soon out of Jennie's sight, but had a happy little corner in his heart, because he had tried to do a kind act. He did not know how much good he had done in making a pleasant day out of a dreary one for a little sick girl.

14. "Mamma," said George, that evening, after he had told her what Jennie said, "papa must give them some money, so they can go back to their home."

15. "No," said his mother; "he can not do that, and they would not wish him to do so; but perhaps

he can help us contrive some way to assist them, so that they can live more comfortably."

16. "I am going to carry Jennie some of the grapes grandpa sent me, to-morrow," said George, turning over the leaves of his geography. "I will put some of my pears into your basket, and go with you," said his mother; "but there is one thing we can always give, and sometimes it does more good than nice things to eat, or even money."

17. "What is that, mamma,—smiles?" asked George, looking up. "Yes," answered his mother; "and it is a good plan to throw in a kind word or two with them when you can."

DEFINITIONS.–1. Dĭs'mal, *gloomy, cheerless.* Wĭsh'ful-ly, *with desire.* 5. Rĭck'et-y, *imperfect, worn out.* 7. Dĭn'ġy, *dark.* 11. Glȧn'çing, *looking about quickly.* 13. Drēar'y, *comfortless, gloomy.* 15. Con-trīve', *to plan.*

EXERCISES.—What is the subject of this lesson? How did George West make the day pleasant for Jennie? What did his mother suggest? What happened next day? What did Jennie tell George about her life? Relate what happened at George's home that evening. What does the lesson teach?

———————

VII. LAZY NED.

1. "'T is royal fun," cried lazy Ned,
    "To coast, upon my fine, new sled,
        And beat the other boys;
    But then, I can not bear to climb
        The tiresome hill, for every time
        It more and more annoys."

2. So, while his schoolmates glided by,
   And gladly tugged uphill, to try
   Another merry race,
Too indolent to share their plays,
Ned was compelled to stand and gaze,
   While shivering in his place.

3. Thus, he would never take the pains
   To seek the prize that labor gains,
   Until the time had passed;
For, all his life, he dreaded still
The silly bugbear of uphill,
   And died a dunce at last.

DEFINITIONS.–1. Roy′al, *excellent, noble*. Cōast, *to slide*.
An-noyṣ′, *troubles.* 2. In′do-lent, *lazy.* 3. Prīze, *a reward.* Bŭḡ′-
beâr, *something frightful.* Dŭnçe, *a silly fellow.*

EXERCISES.—What did Ned like? What did he not like?

VIII. THE MONKEY.

1. The monkey is a very cunning little animal, and is found in many parts of the world.

2. A lady once had a monkey, which had been brought to her as a present. This monkey, like all others, was very fond of mischief and of doing whatever he saw others do.

3. His mistress found him one day sitting on her toilet table, holding in one hand a little china mug with water in it, and in the other her toothbrush, with which he was cleaning his teeth, looking all the time in the glass.

4. Her little daughter, Maria, had a large doll with a very handsome head and face. She one day left this doll in the cradle, and went out of the room. The monkey came in, took the doll in his arms, and jumping upon the wash-stand, he began to wash its face.

5. He first rubbed it all over with soap. Then seizing the towel, he dipped it in the wash bowl, and rubbed it so hard that the doll's face was entirely spoiled, the paint being all washed off.

6. There have been many tales of monkeys who, armed with sticks, have joined together and made war or resisted their enemies with great effect. These are not true, as it is known that in their native state monkeys have no idea of weapons.

7. The sticks and other missiles said to be thrown at travelers as they pass under the branches of trees, are usually the dead branches, etc., accidentally broken off, as the monkeys, with the natural curiosity of their tribe, pass along the tops of trees to watch the actions of the people below.

8. They can, however, be taught to use a stick, and to use it well. Some time ago, two Italians together owned an organ and a monkey, by means of which

they earned their living. During one of their exhibitions, a dog flew at the little monkey, which made its owners very angry.

9. They and the owner of the dog quarreled about it, and at last it was agreed that the dog and the monkey should fight it out; the monkey, because he was smaller, was to be allowed a stick.

10. The monkey was taught what he was to do in the following manner: One of the Italians crawled on his hands and knees, barking like a dog, while the other got on his back, grasped his hair, and beat him about the head with a stick.

11. The monkey looked on with great gravity, and, when the instruction was over, received the stick with the air of a man who knew his work and meant to do it.

12. Everything being settled the dog flew at the monkey with open month. The monkey immediately leaped on his back, and, grasping the dog's ear, beat away at his head with such good will that his adversary speedily gave in. The monkey, however, was not content with a mere victory, but continued pounding at the dog's head until he left him senseless on the ground.

DEFINITIONS.—1. Cŭn′ning, *sly*. 3. Toi′let-tā′ble, *dressing table*. 6. Re-şĭst′ed, *opposed*. 7. Mĭs′sĭleş, *weapons thrown*. 8. Ex-hi-bĭ′tionş, *public shows*. 11. Grăv′i-ty, *seriousness*. In-strŭe′-tion, *lesson*, 12. Sĕnse′less, *without apparent life*.

EXERCISES.—What kind of an animal is a monkey? Where did the lady find the monkey one day? What was he doing? What did he do with Maria's doll? Do monkeys in their native state know how to use sticks as weapons? Can they be taught to use them? Relate the story of the two Italians. What is the meaning of "etc." in the seventh paragraph?

IX. MEDDLESOME MATTY.

1. Oh, how one ugly trick has spoiled
      The sweetest and the best!
   Matilda, though a pleasant child,
      One grievous fault possessed,
   Which, like a cloud before the skies,
   Hid all her better qualities.

2. Sometimes, she'd lift the teapot lid
      To peep at what was in it;
   Or tilt, the kettle, if you did
      But turn your back a minute.
   In vain you told her not to touch,
   Her trick of meddling grew so much.

3. Her grand mamma went out one day,
      And, by mistake, she laid
   Her spectacles and snuffbox gay,
      Too near the little maid;
   "Ah! well," thought she, "I'll try them on,
   As soon as grand mamma is gone."

4. Forthwith, she placed upon her nose
      The glasses large and wide;
   And looking round, as I suppose,
      The snuffbox, too, she spied.
   "Oh, what a pretty box is this!
   I'll open it," said little miss.

5. "I know that grandmamma would say,
      'Don't meddle with it, dear;'
   But then she's far enough away,
      And no one else is near;

Beside, what can there be amiss
In opening such a box as this?"

6. So, thumb and finger went to work
   To move the stubborn lid;
   And, presently, a mighty jerk
   The mighty mischief did;
   For all at once, ah! woeful case!
   The snuff came puffing in her face.

7. Poor eyes, and nose, and mouth, and chin
   A dismal sight presented;
   And as the snuff got further in,
   Sincerely she repented.
   In vain she ran about for ease,
   She could do nothing else but sneeze.

8. She dashed the spectacles away,
   To wipe her tingling eyes;
   And, as in twenty bits they lay,
   Her grandmamma she spies.
   "Heyday! and what's the matter now?"
   Cried grandmamma, with angry brow.

9. Matilda, smarting with the pain,
   And tingling still, and sore,
   Made many a promise to refrain
   From meddling evermore;
   And 't is a fact, as I have heard,
   She ever since has kept her word.

DEFINITIONS. 1. Qual'i-ties, *traits* of character. 2. Měd'-dling, *interfering without right.* 4. Fōrth-wĭth', *at once.* Spīed, *saw.* 5. A-mĭss', *wrong, faulty.* 6. Wōe'fŭl, *sad, sorrowful* 8. Tĭn'gling, *smarting.* 9. Re-frāin', *to keep from.*

EXERCISES.—What did Matilda do? How was she punished? What effect did it have on her?

X. THE GOOD SON.

1. There was once a jeweler, noted for many virtues. One day, the Jewish elders came to him to buy some diamonds, to put upon that part of the dress of their high priest, which the Bible calls an ephod.

2. They told him what they wanted, and offered him a fair price for the diamonds. He replied that he could not let them see the jewels at that moment, and requested them to call again.

3. As they wanted them without delay, and thought that the object of the jeweler was only to increase the price of the diamonds, the elders offered him twice, then three times, as much as they were worth. But he still refused, and they went away in very bad humor.

4. Some hours after, he went to them, and placed before them the diamonds, for which they again offered him the last price they had named; but he said, "I will only accept the first one you offered to me this morning."

5. "Why, then, did you not close with us at once?" asked they in surprise. "When you came," replied he, "my father had the key of the chest, in which the diamonds were kept, and as he was asleep, I should have been obliged to wake him to obtain them.

6. "At his age, a short hour of sleep does him a great deal of good; and for all the gold in the world, I would not be wanting in respect to my father, or take from him a single comfort."

7. The elders, affected by these feeling words, spread their hands upon the jeweler's head, and said, "Thou shalt be blessed of Him who has said, 'Honor thy

father and thy mother;' and thy children shall one day pay thee the same respect and love thou hast shown to thy father."

DEFINITIONS.—1. Jew'el-er, *one who buys and sells precious stones.* Nōt'ed, *well known.* Eld'er, *an officer of the Jewish church.* Eph'od, *part of the dress of a Jewish priest, made of two pieces, one covering the chest and the other the back, united by a girdle.* 2. Dī'a-monds, *precious stones.* 3. Hū'mor, *state of mind, temper.* 5. Clōṣe, *come to an agreement.*

EXERCISES.—Relate the story of the jeweler and his diamonds. What did the elders say to him, when they heard his reason for not giving them the diamonds at first?

XI. TO-MORROW.

Mrs. M. B. Johnson is the authoress of "To-morrow," one of a collection of poems; entitled "Poems of Home Life."

1. A bright, merry boy, with laughing face,
   Whose every motion was full of grace,
   Who knew no trouble and feared no care,
   Was the light of our household—the youngest there.

2. He was too young, this little elf,
   With troublesome questions to vex himself;
   But for many days a thought would rise,
   And bring a shade to his dancing eyes.

3. He went to one whom he thought more wise
   Than any other beneath the skies;
   "Mother,"—O word that makes the home!—
   "Tell me, when will to-morrow come?"

4. "It is almost night," the mother said,
   "And time for my boy to be in bed;
   When you wake up and it's day again,
   It will be to-morrow, my darling, then."

5. The little boy slept through all the night,
   But woke with the first red streak of light;
   He pressed a kiss to his mother's brow,
   And whispered, "Is it to-morrow now?"

6. "No, little Eddie, this is to-day:
   To-morrow is always one night away."
   He pondered a while, but joys came fast,
   And this vexing question quickly passed.

7. But it came again with the shades of night;
   "Will it be to-morrow when it is light?"
   From years to come he seemed care to borrow,
   He tried so hard to catch to-morrow.

8. "You can not catch it, my little Ted;
   Enjoy to-day," the mother said;
   "Some wait for to-morrow through many a year
   It is always coming, but never is here."

DEFINITIONS.—1. House'hŏld, *family, those living in the same house*. 2. Elf, *a small fairy-like person*. Vĕx, *worry, trouble*. Pŏn'dered, *thought anxiously*. A-whīle', *for a short time*.

EXERCISES.—What is meant by "dancing eyes" in the second stanza? What is meant by "the shades of night," in the seventh stanza? Of what name are "Eddie" and "Ted" nicknames? What troubled Eddie? Can you define tomorrow? What did Eddie's mother advise him to do?

XII. WHERE THERE IS A WILL THERE IS A WAY.

1. Henry Bond was about ten years old when his father died. His mother found it difficult to provide for the support of a large family, thus left entirely in her care. By good management, however, she contrived to do so, and also to send Henry, the oldest, to school, and to supply him, for the most part, with such books as he needed.

2. At one time, however, Henry wanted a grammar, in order to join a class in that study, and his mother could not furnish him with the money to buy it. He was very much troubled about it, and went to bed with a heavy heart, thinking what could be done.

3. On waking in the morning, he found that a deep snow had fallen, and the cold wind was blowing furiously. "Ah," said he, "it is an ill wind that blows nobody good."

4. He rose, ran to the house of a neighbor, and offered his service to clear a path around his premises. The offer was accepted. Having completed this work, and received his pay, he went to another place for the same purpose, and then to another, until he had earned enough to buy a grammar.

5. When school commenced, Henry was in his seat, the happiest boy there, ready to begin the lesson in his new book.

6. From that time, Henry, was always the first in all his classes. He knew no such word as fail, but always succeeded in all he attempted. Having the will, he always found the way.

DEFINITIONS.—1. Măn′aġe-ment, *manner of directing things.* 2. Fûr′nish, *to supply.* 3. Fū′ri-oŭs-ly, *violently.* 4. Sẽrv′ĭçe, *labor.* Prĕm′i-seṣ, *grounds around a house.*

XIII. PICCOLA.

By **Celia Laighton Thaxter**, who was born at Portsmouth, N. H., June 29, 1836. Much of her childhood was passed at White Island, one of the Isles of Shoals, off the coast of New Hampshire. "Among the Isles of Shoals," is her most noted work in prose. She published a volume of poems, many of which are favorites with children.

1. Poor, sweet Piccola! Did you hear
   What happened to Piccola, children dear?
   'T is seldom Fortune such favor grants
   As fell to this little maid of France.

2. 'T was Christmas time, and her parents poor
   Could hardly drive the wolf from the door,
   Striving with poverty's patient pain
   Only to live till summer again.

3. No gift for Piccola! sad were they
   When dawned the morning of Christmas day!
   Their little darling no joy might stir;
   St. Nicholas nothing would bring to her!

4. But Piccola never doubted at all
   That something beautiful must befall
   Every child upon Christmas day,
   And so she slept till the dawn was gray.

5. And full of faith, when at last she woke,
   She stole to her shoe as the morning broke;
   Such sounds of gladness filled all the air,
   'T was plain St. Nicholas had been there.

6. In rushed Piccola, sweet, half wild—
   Never was seen such a joyful child—
   "See what the good saint brought!" she cried,
   And mother and father must peep inside.

7. Now such a story I never heard!
   There was a little shivering bird!
   A sparrow, that in at the window flew,
   Had crept into Piccola's tiny shoe!

8. "How good poor Piccola must have been!"
   She cried, as happy as any queen,
   While the starving sparrow she fed and warmed,
   And danced with rapture, she was so charmed.

9. Children, this story I tell to you
   Of Piccola sweet and her bird, is true.
   In the far-off land of France, they say,
   Still do they live to this very day.

DEFINITIONS.—3. Dawned, *began to grow light.* Stūr, *excite.*
4. Be-fall', *happen.* 7. Shĭv'er-ing, *trembling from cold.* Tī'ny,
very small. 8. Răpt'ūre, *great joy.* Chärmed, *greatly.*

EXERCISES.—What is meant by "driving the wolf from the
door"? In the third stanza, what does "St." before Nicholas
mean? Who is St. Nicholas? What did Piccola find in her shoe
on Christmas morning?

XIV. TRUE MANLINESS.

BY MRS. M. O. JOHNSON.—(ADAPTED.)

1. "Please, mother, do sit down and let me try my hand," said Fred Liscom, a bright, active boy twelve years old. Mrs. Liscom, looking pale and worn, was moving languidly about, trying to clear away the breakfast she had scarcely tasted.

2. She smiled, and said, "You, Fred, you wash dishes?" "Yes, indeed, mother," replied Fred; "I should be a poor scholar if I couldn't, when I've seen you do it so many times. Just try me."

3. A look of relief came over his mother's face as she seated herself in her low rocking-chair. Fred washed the dishes, and put them in the closet. He then swept the kitchen, brought up the potatoes from the cellar for the dinner and washed them, and then set out for school.

4. Fred's father was away from home, and as there was some cold meat in the pantry, Mrs. Liscom found it an easy task to prepare dinner. Fred hurried home from school, set the table, and again washed the dishes.

5. He kept on in this way for two or three days, till his mother was able to resume her usual work, and he felt amply rewarded when the doctor, who happened in one day, said, "Well, madam, it's my opinion that you would have been very sick if you had not kept quiet."

6. The doctor did not know how the "quiet" had been secured, nor how the boy's heart bounded at his words. Fred had given up a great deal of what boys

hold dear, for the purpose of helping his mother, coasting and skating being just at this time in perfection.

7. Besides this, his temper and his patience had been severely tried. He had been in the habit of going early to school, and staying to play after it was dismissed.

8. The boys missed him, and their curiosity was excited when he would give no other reason for not coming to school earlier, or staying after school, than that he was a "wanted at home." "I'll tell you," said Tom Barton, "I'll find him out, boys—see if I don't!"

9. So he called for Fred to go to school, and on his way to the side door walked lightly and somewhat nearer the kitchen window than was absolutely needful. Looking in, he saw Fred standing at the table with a dishcloth in his hand.

10. Of course he reported this at school, and various were the greetings poor Fred received at recess. "Well, you're a brave one to stay at home washing dishes." "Girl boy!" "Pretty Bessie!" "Lost your apron, haven't you, Polly!"

11. Fred was not wanting either in spirit or courage, and he was strongly tempted to resent these insults and to fight some of his tormentors. But his consciousness of right and his love for his mother helped him.

12. While he was struggling for self mastery, his teacher appeared at the door of the school-house. Fred caught his eye, and it seemed to look, if it did not say, "Don't give up! Be really brave!" He knew the teacher had heard the insulting taunts of his thoughtless schoolmates.

13. The boys received notice during the day that Fred must not be taunted or teased in any manner. They knew that the teacher meant what he said; and so the brave little boy had no farther trouble.

DEFINITIONS.—1. Lăn′ḡuid-ly, *feebly*. 5. Am′ply, *fully.* O-pĭn′ion, *judgment, belief.* 9. Ab′so-lūte-ly, *wholly, entirely.* 11. Re-ṣent′, *to consider as an injury.* Cŏn′scioŭs-ness, *inward feeling, knowledge of what passes in one's own mind.*

Exercises.—Why did Fred offer to wash the dishes? Was it a disgraceful thing to do? How was he rewarded? How did his schoolmates show their lack of manliness?

XV. TRUE MANLINESS.

(CONCLUDED.)

1. "Fire! fire!" The cry crept out on the still night air, and the fire bells began to ring. Fred was wakened by the alarm and the red light streaming into his room. He dressed himself in a moment, almost, and tapped at the door of his mother's bedroom.

2. "It is Mr. Barton's house, mother. Do let me go," he said in eager, excited tones. Mrs. Liscom thought a moment. He was young, but she could trust him, and she knew how much his heart was in the request.

3. "Yes, you may go," she answered; "but be careful, my boy. If you can help, do so; but do nothing rashly." Fred promised to follow her advice, and hurried to the fire.

4. Mr. and Mrs. Barton were not at home. The house had been left in charge of the servants. The

fire spread with fearful speed, for there was a high wind, and it was found impossible to save the house. The servants ran about, screaming and lamenting, but doing nothing to any purpose.

5. Fred found Tom outside, in safety. "Where is Katy?" he asked. Tom, trembling with terror, seemed to have had no thought but of his own escape. He said, "Katy is in the house!" "In what room?" asked Fred. "In that one," pointing to a window in the upper story.

6. It was no time for words, but for instant, vigorous action. The staircase was already on fire; there was but one way to reach Katy, and that full of danger. The second floor might fall at any moment, and Fred knew it. But he trusted in an arm stronger than his own, and silently sought help and guidance.

7. A ladder was quickly brought, and placed against the house. Fred mounted it, followed by the hired man, dashed in the sash of the window, and pushed his way into the room where the poor child lay nearly suffocated with smoke.

8. He roused her with some difficulty, carried her to the window, and placed her upon the sill. She was instantly grasped by strong arms, and carried down the ladder, Fred following as fast as possible. They had scarcely reached the ground before a crash of falling timbers told them that they had barely escaped with their lives.

9. Tom Barton never forgot the lesson of that night; and he came to believe, and to act upon the belief, in after years, that true manliness is in harmony with gentleness, kindness, and self-denial.

EXERCISES.—Relate the story of the fire. What is meant by "to any purpose," in paragraph four? Did Fred show any lack of manliness when tested? What does this lesson teach?

XVI. THE BROWN THRUSH.

Lucy Larcom, the author of the following poem, was born in 1826, and passed many years of her life as a factory girl at Lowell, Mass.

1. There's a merry brown thrush sitting up in a tree;
   "He's singing to me! he's singing to me!"
And what does he say, little girl, little boy?
   "Oh, the world's running over with joy!
   Don't You hear? Don't you see?
      Hush! look! In my tree
   I'm as happy as happy can be!"

2. And the brown thrush keeps singing, "A nest do
   you see,
 And five eggs hid by me in the juniper tree?
Don't meddle! don't touch! little girl, little boy,
 Or the world will lose some of its joy!
   Now I'm glad! now I'm free!
   And I always shall be,
If you never bring sorrow to me."

3. So the merry brown thrush sings away in the tree,
  To you and to me, to you and to me;
 And he sings all the day, little girl, little boy,
  "Oh, the world's running over with joy!
   But long it won't be,
    Don't you know? Don't you see?
Unless we're as good as can be."

EXERCISES.—What is a thrush? Why was the thrush so happy? Do you think he would have been happy if the little boy or girl had robbed the nest?

XVII. A SHIP IN A STORM.

1. Did you ever go far out upon the great ocean? How beautiful it is to be out at sea, when the sea is smooth and still!

2. Let a storm approach, and the scene is changed. The heavy, black clouds appear in the distance, and throw a deep, deathlike shade over the world of waters.

3. The captain and sailors soon see in the clouds the signs of evil. All hands are then set to work to take in sail.

4. The hoarse notes of the captain, speaking through his trumpet, are echoed from lip to lip among the rigging. Happy will it be, if all is made snug before the gale strikes the vessel.

5. At last, the gale comes like a vast moving mountain of air. It strikes the ship. The vessel heaves and groans under the dreadful weight, and struggles to escape through the foaming waters.

6. If she is far out at sea, she will be likely to ride out the storm in safety. But if the wind is driving

her upon the shore, the poor sailors will hardly escape being dashed upon the rocks, and drowned.

7. Once there was a ship in a storm. Some of her masts were already broken, and her sails lost. While the wind was raging, and the billows were dashing against her, the cry was heard, "A man has fallen overboard!"

8. Quickly was the boat lowered, and she was soon seen bounding on her way over the mountain waves. At one moment, the boat seemed lifted to the skies, and the next, it sank down, and appeared to be lost beneath the waves!

9. At length, the man was found. He was well nigh drowned; but he was taken on board, and now they made for the ship. But the ship rolled so dreadfully, that it seemed certain death to go near her. And now, what should they do?

10. The captain told one of the men to go aloft and throw down a rope. This was made fast to the boat, and when the sea was somewhat calm it was hoisted, and all fell down into the ship with a dreadful crash. It was a desperate way of getting on board; but fortunately no lives were lost.

11. On the dangerous points along our seacoast are lighthouses, which can be seen far out at sea, and serve as guides to ships. Sometimes the fog is so dense that these lights can not be seen, but most lighthouses have great fog bells or fog horns; some of the latter are made to sound by steam, and can be heard for a long distance. These bells and horns are kept sounding as long as the fog lasts.

12. There are also many life-saving stations along the coast where trained men are ready with lifeboats. "When a ship is driven ashore they at once go to the

rescue of those on board, and thus many valuable lives
are saved.

13. Take it all in all, a sailor's life is a very hard one.
Our young friends owe a debt of gratitude to those
whose home is upon the great waters, and who bring
them the luxuries of other countries.

DEFINITIONS.—4. Ĕch′ōed, *sounded again.* Gāle, *a wind
storm.* 5. Hēaveş, *pitches up and down.* 7. Bĭl′lowş, *waves.* 10.
Dĕs′-per-ate, *hopeless.* 11. Fŏg, *watery vapor, mist.* 13. Grăt′i-
tūde, *thankfulness.* Lŭx′ū-rieş, *nice things.*

EXERCISES.—What is this lesson about? When is it dangerous to be at sea? What do sailors then do? In what situation are
they most likely to be saved? Relate the story of the man overboard. Tell about the lighthouses. How are vessels warned of
danger in a fog? What about the life-saving stations? What is
said of a sailor's life?

XVIII. THE SAILOR'S CONSOLATION.

Charles Dibdin, the author, was born at Southampton, England, in
1745. He wrote a number of fine sea songs. He died in 1814.

1. One night came on a hurricane,
    The sea was mountains rolling,
When Barney Buntline turned his quid,
    And said to Billy Bowling:
"A strong norwester's blowing, Bill;
    Hark! don't ye hear it roar now?
Lord help 'em, how I pities all
    Unhappy folks on shore now!

2. "Foolhardy chaps who live in town,
    What danger they are all in,

And now are quaking in their beds,
   For fear the roof shall fall in;
Poor creatures, how they envy us,
   And wish, as I've a notion,
For our good luck, in such a storm,
   To be upon the ocean.

3. "But as for them who're out all day,
   On business from their houses,
And late at night are coming home,
   To cheer the babes and spouses;
While you and I, Bill, on the deck,
   Are comfortably lying,
My eyes! what tiles and chimney pots
   About their heads are flying!

4. "And very often have we heard
   How men are killed and undone
By overturns of carriages,
   By thieves, and fires in London.
We know what risks all landsmen run,
   From noblemen to tailors;
Then, Bill, let us thank Providence
   That you and I are sailors."

DEFINITIONS.–1. Hŭr'ri-€āne, *a violent windstorm.* Quĭd, *a small piece of tobacco.* 2. Fōōl'-här'dy, *reckless.* Quāk'ing, *shaking with fear.* Nō'tion, *idea.* 3. Spouṣ'eṣ, *wives.* Tīleṣ, *thin pieces of baked clay used in roofing houses.* Chĭm'ney-pŏts, *earthenware tops of chimneys.* 4. Un-dòne', *injured, ruined.*

NOTES.—l. "Barney Buntline" and "Billy Bowling" are supposed to be two sailors. "Norwester" is a sailor's name for a northwest storm. 4. "Landsmen" is a term applied by sailors to all who live on shore.

XIX. TWO WAYS OF TELLING A STORY.

By Henry K. Oliver.

1. In one of the most populous cities of New England, a few years ago, a party of lads, all members of the same school, got up a grand sleigh ride. The sleigh was a very large one, drawn by six gray horses.

2. On the following day, as the teacher entered the schoolroom, he found his pupils in high glee, as they chattered about the fun and frolic of their excursion. In answer to some inquiries, one of the lads gave him an account of their trip and its various incidents.

3. As he drew near the end of his story, he exclaimed: "Oh, sir! there was one thing I had almost forgotten. As we were coming home, we saw ahead

of us a queer looking affair in the road. It proved to be a rusty old sleigh, fastened behind a covered wagon, proceeding at a very slow rate, and taking up the whole road.

4. "Finding that the owner was not disposed to turn out, we determined upon a volley of snow-balls and a good hurrah. They produced the right effect, for the crazy machine turned out into the deep snow, and the skinny old pony started on a full trot.

5. "As we passed, some one gave the horse a good crack, which made him run faster than he ever did before, I'll warrant.

6. "With that, an old fellow in the wagon, who was buried up under an old hat, bawled out, 'Why do you frighten my horse?' 'Why don't you turn out, then?' says the driver. So we gave him three rousing cheers more. His horse was frightened again, and ran up against a loaded wagon, and, I believe, almost capsized the old creature—and so we left him."

7. "Well, boys," replied the teacher, "take your seat", and I will tell you a story, and all about a sleigh ride, too. Yesterday afternoon a very venerable old clergyman was on his way from Boston to Salem, to pass the rest of the winter at the house of his son. That he might be prepared for journeying in the following spring he took with him his wagon, and for the winter his sleigh, which he fastened behind the wagon.

8. "His sight and hearing were somewhat blunted by age, and he was proceeding very slowly; for his horse was old and feeble, like his owner. He was suddenly disturbed by loud hurrahs from behind, and by a furious pelting of balls of snow and ice upon the top of his wagon.

9. "In his alarm he dropped his reins, and his horse began to run away. In the midst of the old man's trouble, there rushed by him, with loud shouts, a large party of boys, in a sleigh drawn by six horses. 'Turn out! turn out, old fellow!' 'Give us the road!' 'What will you take for your pony?' 'What's the price of oats, old man?' were the various cries that met his cars.

10. "'Pray, do not frighten my horse!' exclaimed the infirm driver. 'Turn out, then! turn out!' was the answer, which was followed by repeated cracks and blows from the long whip of the 'grand sleigh,' with showers of snowballs, and three tremendous hurrahs from the boys.

11. "The terror of the old man and his horse was increased, and the latter ran away with him, to the great danger of his life. He contrived, however, to stop his horse just in season to prevent his being dashed against a loaded wagon. A short distance brought him to the house of his son. That son, boys, is your instructor, and that 'old fellow,' was your teacher's father!"

12. When the boys perceived how rude and unkind their conduct appeared from another point of view, they were very much ashamed of their thoughtlessness, and most of them had the manliness to apologize to their teacher for what they had done.

DEFINITIONS.—1. Pŏp'ū-loŭs, *full of inhabitants.* 2. Ex-cûr'-sion, *a pleasure trip.* In'çi-dents, *things that happen, events.* 5. Wạr'rant, *to declare with assurance.* 6. Cap-sīzed', *upset.* 7. Vĕn'er-a-ble, *deserving of honor and respect.* 8. Blŭnt'ed, *dulled.*

Exercises.—Repeat the boys' story of the sleigh ride. The teacher's story. Were the boys ill-natured or only thoughtless? Is thoughtlessness any excuse for rudeness or unkindness?

XX. FREAKS OF THE FROST.

By **Hannah Flagg Gould**, who was born at Lancaster, Vermont, in 1789. She published several volumes of poems (one for children) and one collection of prose articles, entitled "Gathered Leaves."

1. The Frost looked forth one still, clear night,
   And whispered, "Now I shall be out of sight;
   So through the valley and over the height
      In silence I'll take my way;
   I will not go on, like that blustering train,
   The wind and the snow, the hail and the rain,
   Who make so much bustle and noise in vain,
      But I'll be as busy as they."

2. Then he flew to the mountain, and powdered its
         crest;
   He lit on the trees, and their boughs he dressed
   In diamond beads; and over the breast
      Of the quivering lake, he spread
   A coat of mail, that it need not fear
   The downward point of many a spear,
      That he hung on its margin, far and near,
   Where a rock could rear its head.

3. He went to the windows of those who slept,
   And over each pane, like a fairy, crept;
   Wherever he breathed, wherever he stepped,
      By the light of the morn were seen
   Most beautiful things; there were flowers and trees;
   There were bevies of birds, and swarms of bees;
   There were cities with temples and towers, and
         these
      All pictured in silver sheen.

4. But he did one thing that was hardly fair;
  He peeped in the cupboard, and, finding there
  That all had forgotten for him to prepare,
    "Now just to set them a-thinking,
  I'll bite this basket of fruit," said he,
  "This costly pitcher I'll burst in three;
  And the glass of water they've left for me
    Shall 'tchick!' to tell them I'm drinking."

DEFINITIONS.—l. Blŭs′ter-ing, *being noisy and loud.* Bŭs′tle,
stir. 2. Crĕst, *the top.* Quĭv′er-ing, *trembling, shaking.* Mär′ġin,
edge, border. 3. Bĕv′ieṣ, *flocks.* Pĭe′tūred, *painted.* Sheen, *brightness, splendor of appearance.*

EXERCISES.—What did the frost say? What did he do to the
mountain? The trees? The lake? What is a "coat of mail"? What
did he do to the window? The pitcher?

———————————

XXI. WASTE NOT, WANT NOT.

1. *Mr. Jones.* Boys, if you have nothing to do, will
you unpack these parcels for me?

2. The two parcels were exactly alike, both of them
well tied up with good whipcord. Ben took his parcel
to the table, and began to examine the knot, and then
to untie it.

3. John took the other parcel, and tried first at one
corner, and then at the other, to pull off the string. But
the cord had been too well secured, and he only drew
the knots tighter.

4. *John.* I wish these people would not tie up their
parcels so tightly, as if they were never to be undone.
Why, Ben, how did you get yours undone? What is

in your parcel? I wonder what is in mine! I wish I could get the string off. I will cut it.

5. *Ben.* Oh, no, do not cut it, John! Look, what a nice cord this is, and yours is the same. It is a pity to cut it.

6. *John.* Pooh! what signifies a bit of pack thread?

7. *Ben.* It is whipcord.

8. *John.* Well, whipcord then! what signifies a bit of whipcord? You can get a piece of whipcord twice as long as that for three cents; and who cares for three cents? Not I, for one. So, here it goes.

9. So he took out his knife, and cut it in several places.

10. *Mr. Jones.* Well, my boys, have you undone the parcels for me?

11. *John.* Yes, sir; here is the parcel.

12. *Ben.* And here is my parcel, father, and here is also the string.

13. *Mr. Jones.* You may keep the string, Ben.

14. *Ben.* Thank you, sir. What excellent whipcord it is!

15. *Mr. Jones.* And you, John, may keep your string, too, if it will be of any use to you.

16. *John.* It will be of no use to me, thank you, sir.

17. *Mr. Jones.* No, I am afraid not, if this is it.

18. A few weeks after this, Mr. Jones gave each of his sons a new top.

19. *John.* How is this, Ben? These tops have no strings. What shall we do for strings?

20. *Ben.* I have a string that will do very well for mine. And he pulled it out of his pocket.

21. *John.* Why, if that is not the whipcord! I wish I had saved mine.

22. A few days afterward, there was a shooting match, with bows and arrows, among the lads. The prize was a fine bow and arrows, to be given to the best marksman. "Come, come," said Master Sharp, "I am within one inch of the mark. I should like to see who will go nearer."

23. John drew his bow, and shot. The arrow struck within a quarter of an inch of Master Sharp's. "Shoot away," said Sharp; "but you must understand the rules. We settled them before you came. You are to have three shots with your own arrows. Nobody is to borrow or lend. So shoot away."

24. John seized his second arrow; "If I have any luck," said he;—but just as he pronounced the word "luck," the string broke, and the arrow fell from his hands.

25. *Master Sharp.* There! It is all over with you.

26. *Ben.* Here is my bow for him, and welcome.

27. *Master Sharp.* No, no, sir; that is not fair. Did you not hear the rules? There is to be no lending.

28. It was now Ben's turn to make his trial. His first arrow missed the mark; the second was exactly as near as John's first. Before venturing the last arrow, Ben very prudently examined the string of his bow; and, as he pulled it to try its strength, it snapped.

29. Master Sharp clapped his hands and danced for joy. But his dancing suddenly ceased, when careful Ben drew out of his pocket an excellent piece of cord, and began to tie it to the bow.

30. "The everlasting whipcord, I declare!" cried John. "Yes," said Ben, "I put it in my pocket today, because I thought I might want it."

31. Ben's last arrow won the prize; and when the bow and arrows were handed to him, John said, "How valuable that whipcord has been to you, Ben. I'll take care how I waste anything hereafter."

DEFINITIONS,—2. Ex-ăm'ĭne, *to look at carefully.* 6. Sĭg'nifĭeş, *to be important.* 22. Märks'man, *one who shoots well.* 28. Pru'dent-ly, *with proper caution.* 29. Cēased, *stopped.* 30. Ever-lȧst'ing, *lasting always.*

EXERCISES.—What is this lesson designed to teach? Which of the boys preserved his whipcord? What good did it do him? What did the other boy do with his? What was the consequence? What did he learn from it?

XXII. JEANNETTE AND JO.

BY MARY MAPES DODGE.

1. Two girls I know—Jeannette and Jo,
    And one is always moping;
The other lassie, come what may,
    Is ever bravely hoping.

2. Beauty of face and girlish grace
    Are theirs, for joy or sorrow;
Jeannette takes brightly every day,
    And Jo dreads each to-morrow.

3. One early morn they watched the dawn—
    I saw them stand together;
Their whole day's sport, 't was very plain,
    Depended on the weather.

4. "'T will storm!" cried Jo. Jeannette spoke low:
        "Yes, but 't will soon be over."
    And, as she spoke, the sudden shower
        Came, beating down the clover.

5. "I told you so!" cried angry Jo:
        "It always is a-raining!"
    Then hid her face in dire despair,
        Lamenting and complaining.

6. But sweet Jeannette, quite hopeful yet,—
        I tell it to her honor,—
    Looked up and waited till the sun
        Came streaming in upon her.

7. The broken clouds sailed off in crowds,
        Across a sea of glory.
    Jeannette and Jo ran, laughing, in—
        Which ends my simple story.

8. Joy is divine. Come storm, come shine,
        The hopeful are the gladdest;
    And doubt and dread, children, believe
        Of all things are the saddest.

9. In morning's light, let youth be bright;
        Take in the sunshine tender;
    Then, at the close, shall life's decline
        Be full of sunset splendor.

10. And ye who fret, try, like Jeannette,
        To shun all weak complaining;
    And not, like Jo, cry out too soon—
        "It always is a-raining!"

XXIII. THE LION.

1. The lion is often called the "king of beasts," His height varies from three to four feet, and he is from six to nine feet long. His coat is of it yellowish brown or tawny color, and about his neck is a great shaggy mane which gives his head a majestic appearance.

2. The strength of the lion is so great that he can easily crush the skulls of such animals as the horse or ox with one blow of his paw. No one who has not seen the teeth of a full grown lion taken out of their sockets can have any idea of their real size; one of them forms a good handful, and might easily be mistaken for a small elephant's tooth.

3. The home of the lion is in the forests of Asia and Africa, where he is a terror to man and beast. He generally lies concealed during the day, but as darkness comes on he prowls about where other ani-

mals are accustomed to go for food or drink, and springs upon them unawares, with a roar that sounds like the rumble of thunder.

4. The lion sometimes lives to a great age. One by the name of Pompey died at London, in the year 1760, at the age of seventy years. If taken when young the lion can be tamed, and will even show marks of kindness to his keeper.

5. In a menagerie at Brussels, there was a cell where a large lion, called Danco, used to be kept. The cell happened to be in need of repair, and the keeper, whose name was William, desired a carpenter to come and mend it. The carpenter came, but was so afraid of the lion, that he would not go near the cell alone.

6. So William entered the cell, and led the lion to the upper part of it, while the other part was refitting. He played with the lion for some time; but, at last, being wearied, both he and the lion fell asleep. The carpenter went on with his work, and when he had finished he called out for William to come and see it.

7. He called again and again, but no William answered. The poor carpenter began to be frightened, lest the lion had made his dinner of the keeper, or else crushed him with his great paws. He crept round to the upper part of the cell, and there, looking through the railing, he saw the lion and William sleeping side by side as contentedly as two little brothers.

8. He was so astonished that he uttered a loud cry. The lion, awakened by the noise, stared at the carpenter with an eye of fury, and then placing his paw on the breast of his keeper, as if to say, "Touch

him if you dare," the heroic beast lay down to sleep again. The carpenter was dreadfully alarmed, and, not knowing how he could rouse William, he ran out and related what he had seen.

9. Some people came, and, opening the door of the cell, Contrived to awaken the keeper, who, rubbing his eyes, quietly looked around him, and expressed himself very well satisfied with his nap. He took the lion's paw, shook it kindly, and then retired uninjured from the cell.

DEFINITIONS.—1. Ma-jĕs′tic, *royal, noble*. 3. Prowls, *wanders in search of prey.* Un-a-wâres′, *unexpectedly.* Rŭm′ble, *a low heavy sound.* 5. Men-ăg′er-ie, *a collection of wild animals.* 6. Re-fĭt′ting, *repairing.* 8. He-rō′-ic, *bold.*

EXERCISES.—Describe the lion's appearance. What is said of his strength? His teeth? Describe the lion's home and habits. To what age do lions live? Can they be tamed? Relate the story about the lion Danco.

XXIV. STRAWBERRIES.

By **John Townsend Trowbridge**, who was born at Ogden, N. Y., in 1827. He is a well-known author, and has written much for children both in poetry and prose.

1. Little Pearl Honeydew, six years old,
From her bright ear parted the curls of gold;
And laid her head on the strawberry bed,
To hear what the red-cheeked berries said.

2. Their cheeks were blushing, their breath was sweet,
She could almost hear their little hearts beat;
And the tiniest, lisping, whispering sound
That ever you heard, came up from the ground.

3. "Little friends," she said, "I wish I knew
   How it is you thrive on sun and dew!"
   And this is the story the berries told
   To little Pearl Honeydew, six years old.

4. "You wish you knew? And so do we.
   But we can't tell you, unless it be
   That the same Kind Power that cares for you
   Takes care of poor little berries, too.

5. "Tucked up snugly, and nestled below
   Our coverlid of wind-woven snow,
   We peep and listen, all winter long,
   For the first spring day and the bluebird's song.

6. "When the swallows fly home to the old brown
       shed,
   And the robins build on the bough overhead,
   Then out from the mold, from the darkness and
       cold,
   Blossom and runner and leaf unfold.

7. "Good children, then, if they come near,
   And hearken a good long while, may hear
   A wonderful tramping of little feet,—
   So fast we grow in the summer heat.

8. "Our clocks are the flowers; and they count the
       hours
   Till we can mellow in suns and showers,
   With warmth of the west wind and heat of the
       south,
   A ripe red berry for a ripe red month.

9.   "Apple blooms whiten, and peach blooms fall,
        And roses are gay by the garden wall,
        Ere the daisy's dial gives the sign
        That we may invite little Pearl to dine.

10. "The days are longest, the month is June,
        The year is nearing its golden noon,
        The weather is fine, and our feast is spread
        With a green cloth and berries red.

11. "Just take us betwixt your finger and thumb,
        And quick, oh, quick! for, see! there come
        Tom on all fours, and Martin the man,
        And Margaret, picking as fast as they can.

12. "Oh, dear! if you only knew how it shocks
        Nice berries like us to be sold by the box,
        And eaten by strangers, and paid for with pelf,
        You would surely take pity, and eat us yourself!"

13. And this is the story the small lips told
        To dear Pearl Honeydew, six years old,
        When she laid her head on the strawberry bed
        To hear what the red-cheeked berries said.

DEFINITIONS.—3. Thrīve, *to grow well, to flourish.* 5. Nĕs'tled, *gathered closely together.* 6. Mōld, *fine, soft earth.* Rŭn'ner, *a slender branch running along the ground.* 8. Mĕl'lōw, *to ripen.* 9. Dī'al, *the face of a timepiece.* 10. Fēast, *a festive or joyous meal, a banquet.* 12. Pĕlf, *money.*

EXERCISES.—What did little Pearl ask of the strawberries? What did they reply? Can you tell what name is given to this kind of story?

XVV. HARRY'S RICHES.

1. One day, our little Harry spent the morning with his young playmate, Johnny Crane, who lived in a fine house, and on Sundays rode to church in the grandest carriage to be seen in all the country round.

2. When Harry returned home, he said, "Mother, Johnny has money in both pockets!"

3. "Has he, dear?"

4. "Yes, ma'am; and he says he could get ever so much more if he wanted it."

5. "Well, now, that's very pleasant for him," I returned, cheerfully, as a reply was plainly expected. "Very pleasant; don't you think so?"

6. "Yes, ma'am; only—"

7. "Only what, Harry?"

8. "Why, he has a big popgun, and a watch, and a hobbyhorse, and lots of things." And Harry looked up at my face with a disconsolate stare.

9. "Well, my boy, what of that?"

10. "Nothing, mother," and the telltale tears sprang to his eyes, "only I guess we are very poor, aren't we?"

11. "No, indeed, Harry, we are very far from being poor. We are not so rich as Mr. Crane's family, if that is what you mean."

12. "O mother!" insisted the little fellow, "I do think we are very poor; anyhow, I am!"

13. "O Harry!" I exclaimed, reproachfully.

14. "Yes, ma'am I am," he sobbed; "I have scarcely any thing—I mean anything that's worth money—except things to eat and wear, and I'd have to have them anyway."

15. "Have to have them?" I echoed, at the same time laying my sewing upon the table, so that I might reason with him on that point; "do you not know, my son—"

16. Just then Uncle Ben looked up from the paper he had been reading: "Harry," said he, "I want to find out something about eyes; so, if you will let me have yours, I will give you a dollar apiece for them."

17. "For my eyes!" exclaimed Harry, very much astonished.

18. "Yes," resumed Uncle Ben, quietly, "for your eyes. I will give you chloroform, so it will not hurt you in the least, and you shall have a beautiful glass pair for nothing, to wear in their place. Come, a dollar apiece, cash down! What do you say? I will take them out as quick as a wink."

19. "Give you my eyes, uncle!" cried Harry, looking wild at the very thought, "I think not." And the startled little fellow shook his head defiantly.

20. "Well, five, ten, twenty dollars, then." Harry shook his head at every offer.

21. "No, sir! I wouldn't let you have them for a thousand dollars! What could I do without my eyes? I couldn't see mother, nor the baby, nor the flowers, nor the horses, nor anything," added Harry, growing warmer and warmer.

22. "I will give you two thousand," urged Uncle Ben, taking a roll of bank notes out of his pocket. Harry, standing at a respectful distance, shouted that he never would do any such thing.

23. "Very well," continued the uncle, with a serious air, at the same time writing something in his notebook, "I can't afford to give you more than two

thousand dollars, so I shall have to do without your eyes; but," he added, "I will tell you what I will do, I will give you twenty dollars if you will let me put a few drops from this bottle in your ears. It will not hurt, but it will make you deaf. I want to try some experiments with deafness, you see. Come quickly, now! Here are the twenty dollars all ready for you."

24. "Make me deaf!" shouted Harry, without even looking at the gold pieces temptingly displayed upon the table. "I guess you will not do that, either. Why, I couldn't hear a single word if I were deaf, could I?"

25. "Probably not," replied Uncle Ben. So, of course, Harry refused again. He would never give up his hearing, he said, "no, not for three thousand dollars."

26. Uncle Ben made another note in his book, and then came out with large bids for "a right arm," then "left arm," "hands," "feet," "nose," finally ending with an offer of ten thousand dollars for "mother," and five thousand for "the baby."

27. To all of these offers Harry shook his head, his eyes flashing, and exclamations of surprise and in- dignation bursting from his lips. At last, Uncle Ben said he must give up his experiments, for Harry's prices were entirely too high.

28. "Ha! ha!" laughed the boy, exultingly, and he folded his dimpled arms and looked as if to say, "I'd like to see the man who could pay them!"

29. "Why, Harry, look here!" exclaimed Uncle Ben, peeping into his notebook, "here is a big addi- tion sum, I tell you!" He added the numbers, and they amounted to thirty-two thousand dollars.

30. "There, Harry," said Uncle Ben, "don't you think you are foolish not to accept some of my offers?" "No, sir, I don't," answered Harry, resolutely. "Then," said Uncle Ben, "you talk of being poor, and by your own showing you have treasures for which you will not take thirty-two thousand dollars. What do you say to that?"

31. Harry didn't know exactly what to say. So he blushed for a second, and just then tears came rolling down his cheeks, and he threw his chubby arms around my neck. "Mother," he whispered, "isn't God good to make everybody so rich?"

DEFINITIONS.—8. Dis-€ŏn'so-late, *filled with grief.* 13. Re-prōach'fụl-ly, *with censure or reproof.* 18. Chlō'ro-fôrm, *an oily liquid, the vapor of which causes insensibility.* 19. Stärt'led, *shocked.* De-fī'ant-ly, *daringly.* 23. Af-fôrd', *to be able to pay for.* Ex-pĕr'i-ments, *acts performed to discover some truth.* 27. Ex-€la-mā'tionṣ, *expressions of surprise, anger, etc.* 28. Ex-ŭlt'-ing-ly, *in a triumphant manner.* 30. Trĕaṣ'ūreṣ, *things which are very much valued.*

XXVI. IN TIME'S SWING.

BY LUCY LARCOM.

1. Father Time, your footsteps go
   Lightly as the falling snow.
   In your swing I'm sitting, see!
   Push me softly; one, two; three,
   Twelve times only. Like a sheet,
   Spread the snow beneath my feet.
   Singing merrily, let me swing
   Out of winter into spring.

2. Swing me out, and swing me in!
   Trees are bare, but birds begin
   Twittering to the peeping leaves,
   On the bough beneath the eaves.
   Wait,—one lilac bud I saw.
   Icy hillsides feel the thaw.
   April chased off March to-day;
   Now I catch a glimpse of May.

3. Oh, the smell of sprouting grass!
   In a blur the violets pass.
   Whispering from the wildwood come
   Mayflower's breath and insect's hum.
   Roses carpeting the ground;
   Thrushes, orioles, warbling sound:—
   Swing me low, and swing me high,
   To the warm clouds of July.

4. Slower now, for at my side
   White pond lilies open wide.
   Underneath the pine's tall spire
   Cardinal blossoms burn like fire.
   They are gone; the golden-rod
   Flashes from the dark green sod.
   Crickets in the grass I hear;
   Asters light the fading year.

5. Slower still! October weaves
   Rainbows of the forest leaves.
   Gentians fringed, like eyes of blue,
   Glimmer out of sleety dew.
   Meadow green I sadly miss:
   Winds through withered sedges hiss.
   Oh, 't is snowing, swing me fast,
   While December shivers past!

6. Frosty-bearded Father Time,
Stop your footfall on the rime!
Hard you push, your hand is rough;
You have swung me long enough.
"Nay, no stopping," say you? Well,
Some of your best stories tell,
While you swing me—gently, do!—
From the Old Year to the New.

DEFINITIONS.—2. Twĭt′ter-ing, *making a succession of small, chirping noises.* Glĭmpse, *a short, hurried view.* 3. Blûr, *a dim, confused appearance.* 6. Rīme, *whitefrost, hoarfrost.*

XXVII. HARRY AND HIS DOG.

1. "Beg, Frisk, beg," said little Harry, as he sat on an inverted basket, at his grandmother's door, eating, with great satisfaction, a porringer of bread and milk. His little sister Annie, who had already dispatched her breakfast, sat on the ground opposite to him, now twisting her flowers into garlands, and now throwing them away.

2. "Beg, Frisk, beg!" repeated Harry, holding a bit of bread just out of the dog's reach; and the obedient Frisk squatted himself on his hind legs, and held up his fore paws, waiting for master Harry to give him the tempting morsel.

3. The little boy and the little dog were great friends. Frisk loved him dearly, much better than he did any-one else; perhaps, because he recollected that Harry was his earliest and firmest friend during a time of great trouble.

4. Poor Frisk had come as a stray dog to Milton, the place where Harry lived. If he could have told his own story, it would probably have been a very pitiful one, of kicks and cuffs, of hunger and foul weather.

5. Certain it is, he made his appearance at the very door where Harry was now sitting, in miserable plight, wet, dirty, and half starved; and that there he met Harry, who took a fancy to him, and Harry's grandmother, who drove him off with a broom.

6. Harry, at length, obtained permission for the little dog to remain as a sort of outdoor pensioner, and fed him with stray bones and cold potatoes, and such things as he could get for him. He also provided him with a little basket to sleep in, the very same which, turned up, afterward served Harry for a seat.

7. After a while, having proved his good qualities by barking away a set of pilferers, who were making an attack on the great pear tree, he was admitted into the house, and became one of its most vigilant and valued inmates. He could fetch or carry either by land or water; would pick up a thimble or a ball of cotton, if little Annie should happen to drop them; or take Harry's dinner to school for him with perfect honesty.

8. "Beg, Frisk, beg!" said Harry, and gave him, after long waiting, the expected morsel. Frisk was satisfied, but Harry was not. The little boy, though a good-humored fellow in the main, had turns of naughtiness, which were apt to last him all day, and this promised to prove one of his worst. It was a holiday, and in the afternoon his cousins, Jane and William, were to come and see him and Annie; and

the pears were to be gathered, and the children were to have a treat.

9. Harry, in his impatience, thought the morning would never be over. He played such pranks—buffeting Frisk, cutting the curls off of Annie's doll, and finally breaking his grandmother's spectacles—that before his visitors arrived, indeed, almost immediately after dinner, he contrived to be sent to bed in disgrace.

10. Poor Harry! there he lay, rolling and kicking, while Jane, and William, and Annie were busy about the fine, mellow Windsor pears. William was up in the tree, gathering and shaking; Annie and Jane catching them in their aprons, and picking them up from the ground; now piling them in baskets, and now eating the nicest and ripest; while Frisk was barking gayly among them, as if he were catching Windsor pears, too!

11. Poor Harry! He could hear all this glee and merriment through the open window as he lay in

bed. The storm of passion having subsided, there he lay weeping and disconsolate, a grievous sob bursting forth every now and then, as he heard the loud peals of childish laughter, and as he thought how he should have laughed, and how happy he should have been, had he not forfeited all this pleasure by his own bad conduct.

12. He wondered if Annie would not be so good-natured as to bring him a pear. All on a sudden, he heard a little foot on the stair, pitapat, and he thought she was coming. Pitapat came the foot, nearer and nearer, and at last a small head peeped, half afraid, through the half-open door.

13. But it was not Annie's head; it was Frisk's— poor Frisk, whom Harry had been teasing and tormenting all the morning, and who came into the room wagging his tail, with a great pear in his mouth; and, jumping upon the bed, He laid it in the little boy's hand.

14. Is not Frisk a fine, grateful fellow? and does he not deserve a share of Harry's breakfast, whether he begs for it or not? And little Harry will remember from the events of this day that kindness, even though shown to a dog, will always be rewarded; and that ill nature and bad temper are connected with nothing but pain and disgrace.

DEFINITIONS.—1. In-vĕrt′ed, *turned upside down.* Por′rin-ġer, *a small metallic dish.* 3. Rĕc-ol-lĕct′ed, *brought back to mind.* 5. Plīght, *condition.* 6. Pĕn′sion-er, *one who is supported by others.* 7. Pĭl′fer-erṣ, *those who steal little things.* Vĭg′i-lant, *watchful.* In′timātes, *those living in the same house.* 8. Hŏl′i-dāy, *a day of amusement.* 9. Bŭf′fet-ing, *striking with the hand.* 11. Sub-sīd′ed, *become quiet.* Fôr′feit-ed, *lost.* 14. Con-nect′ed, *united, have a close relation.*

XXVIII. THE VOICE OF THE GRASS.

By Sarah Roberts.

1. Here I come, creeping, creeping, everywhere;
    By the dusty roadside,
    On the sunny hillside,
    Close by the noisy brook,
    In every shady nook,
  I come creeping, creeping, everywhere.

2. Here I come, creeping, creeping everywhere;
    All round the open door,
    Where sit the aged poor,
    Here where the children play,
    In the bright and merry May,
  I come creeping, creeping, everywhere.

3. Here I come, creeping, creeping, everywhere;
    You can not see me coming,
    Nor hear my low, sweet humming,
    For in the starry night,
    And the glad morning light,
  I come, quietly creeping, everywhere.

4. Here I come, creeping, creeping, everywhere;
    More welcome than the flowers,
    In summer's pleasant hours;
    The gentle cow is glad,
    And the merry birds not sad,
  To see me creeping, creeping, everywhere.

5. Here I come, creeping, creeping, everywhere;
  When you're numbered with the dead,
  In your still and narrow bed,
  In the happy spring I'll come,
  And deck your narrow home,
Creeping, silently creeping, everywhere.

6. Here I come, creeping, creeping, everywhere;
  My humble song of praise,
  Most gratefully I raise,
  To Him at whose command
  I beautify the land,
Creeping, silently creeping, everywhere.

XXIX. THE EAGLE.

1. The eagle seems to enjoy a kind of supremacy over the rest of the inhabitants of the air. Such is the loftiness of his flight, that he often soars in the sky beyond the reach of the naked eye, and such is his strength that he has been known to carry away children in his talons. But many of the noble qualities imputed to him are rather fanciful than true.

2. He has been described as showing a lofty independence, which makes him disdain to feed on anything that is not slain by his own strength. But Alexander Wilson, the great naturalist, says that he has seen an eagle feasting on the carcass of a horse. The eagle lives to a great age. One at Vienna is stated to have died after a confinement of one hundred and four years.

3. There are several species of the eagle. The golden eagle, which is one of the largest, is nearly four feet from the point of the beak to the end of the tail. He is found in most parts of Europe, and is also met with in America. High rocks and ruined and lonely towers are the places which he chooses for his abode. His nest is composed of sticks and rushes. The tail feathers are highly valued as ornaments by the American Indians.

4. The most interesting species is the bald-eagle, as this is an American bird, and the adopted emblem of our country. He lives chiefly upon fish, and is found in the neighborhood of the sea, and along the shores and cliffs of our large lakes and rivers.

5. According to the description given by Wilson, he depends, in procuring his food, chiefly upon the labors of others. He watches the fish hawk as he dives into the sea for his prey, and darting down upon him as he rises, forces him to relinquish his victim, and then seizes it before it again reaches the water.

6. One of the most notable species is the harpy-eagle. This is said to be bold and strong, and to attack beasts, and even man himself. He is fierce, quarrelsome, and sullen, living alone in the deepest forests. He is found chiefly in South America.

DEFINITIONS.—1. Su-prĕm′a-çy, *highest authority.* Sōarṣ, *flies aloft.* Im-pūt′ed, *ascribed to.* 2. Lŏft′y, *haughty, dignified.* Diṣ-dāin′, *to scorn.* Cär′eass, *the dead body of an animal.* 3. Spē′-ciēṣ, *classes.* 4. In′ter-ĕst-ing, *engaging the attention.* A-dŏpt′ed, *selected, chosen.* Em′blem, *that which is supposed to resemble some other thing in certain qualities, and is used to represent it.* 5. Re-lĭn′quish, *to give up.* 6. Nōt′a-ble, *worthy of notice.* Sŭl′len, *gloomily angry and silent.*

XXX. THE OLD EAGLE TREE.

1. In a distant field, stood a large tulip tree, apparently of a century's growth, and one of the most gigantic. It looked like the father of the surrounding forest. A single tree of huge dimensions, standing all alone, is a sublime object.

2. On the top of this tree, an old eagle, commonly called the "Fishing Eagle," had built her nest every year, for many years, and, undisturbed, had raised her young. A remarkable place to choose, as she procured her food from the ocean, and this tree stood full ten miles from the seashore. It had long been known as the "Old Eagle Tree."

3. On a warm, sunny day, the workmen were hoeing corn in an adjoining field. At a certain hour of the day, the old eagle was known to set off for the seaside, to gather food for her young. As she this day returned with a large fish in her claws, the workmen surrounded the tree, and, by yelling and hooting, and throwing stones, so scared the poor bird that she dropped her fish, and they carried it off in triumph.

4. The men soon dispersed, but Joseph sat down under a hush near by, to watch, and to bestow unavailing pity. The bird soon returned to her nest, without food. The eaglets at once set up a cry for food, so shrill, so clear, and so clamorous that the boy was greatly moved.

5. The parent bird seemed to try to soothe them; but their appetites were too keen, and it was all in vain. She then perched herself on a limb near them, and looked down into the nest in a manner that seemed to say, "I know not what to do next."

6. Her indecision was but momentary; again she poised herself, uttered one or two sharp notes, as if telling them to a "lie still," balanced her body, spread her wings, and was away again for the sea.

7. Joseph was determined to see the result. His eye followed her till she grew small, smaller, a mere speck in the sky, and then disappeared. What boy has not thus watched the flight of the bird of his country!

8. She was gone nearly two hours, about double her usual time for a voyage, when she again returned, on a slow, weary wing, flying uncommonly low, in order to have a heavier atmosphere to sustain her, with another fish in her talons.

9. On nearing the field, she made a circuit round it, to see if her enemies were again there. Finding the coast clear, she once more reached the tree, drooping, faint, and weary, and evidently nearly exhausted. Again the eaglets set up their cry, which was soon hushed by the distribution of a dinner, such as, save the cooking, a king might admire.

10. "Glorious bird!" cried the boy, "what a spirit!" Other birds can fly more swiftly, others can sing more sweetly, others scream more loudly; but what other bird, when persecuted and robbed, when weary, when discouraged, when so far from the sea, would do this?

11. "Glorious bird! I will learn a lesson from thee to-day. I will never forget, hereafter, that when the spirit is determined it can do almost anything. Others would have drooped, and hung the head, and mourned over the cruelty of man, and sighed over the wants of the nestlings; but thou, by at once recovering the loss, hast forgotten all."

12. "I will learn of thee, noble bird! I will remember this. I will set my mark high. I will try to do something, and to be something in the world; I will never yield to discouragements."

DEFINITIONS.—1. Cĕn′tū-ry, *the space of a hundred years.* Gī-ḡăn′tic, *very large.* Dĭ-mĕn′sions, *size.* Sub-līme′, *grand, noble.* 4. Dis-pērsed′, *scattered.* Un-a-vāil′ing, *useless.* Ea′glets, *young eagles.* Clăm′or-oŭs, *loud, noisy.* 6. In-de-çĭs′ion, *want of fixed purpose.* Mō′ment-a-ry, *for a single moment.* 9. Cīr′cuit, *movement round in a circle.* Ex-hạust′ed, *wholly tired.* 11. Nĕst′-lings, *young birds in the nest.*

Exercises.—Relate the story of the "Old Eagle Tree." What lesson was taught the boy who watched the eagle's actions?

XXXI. ALPINE SONG.

William W. Story, the author, was born in Salem, Mass., in 1819. His writings in poetry and prose are well known, and he also gained distinction in his profession as a sculptor.

1. With alpenstock and knapsack light,
        I wander o'er hill and valley;
    I climb the snow peak's flashing height,
        And sleep in the sheltered chalet,—
    Free in heart—happy and free—
    This is the summer life for me.

2. The city's dust I leave behind
        For the keen, sweet air of the mountain,
    The grassy path by the wild rose lined,
        The gush of the living fountain,—
    Free in heart—happy and free—
    This is the summer life for me.

3. High above me snow clouds rise,
 In the early morning gleaming;
And the patterned valley beneath me lies
 Softly in sunshine dreaming,—
Free in heart—happy and free—
This is the summer life for me.

4. The bells of wandering herds I list,
 Chiming in upland meadows;
How sweet they sound, as I lie at rest
 Under the dark pine shadows—
Glad in heart—happy and free—
This is the summer life for me.

DEFINITIONS.—1. Al'pen-stŏck, *a long staff, pointed with iron, used in traveling among the Alps.* Knăp'săck, *a leather sack for carrying food or clothing, borne on the back.* Cha-let' (pro. shă-lā'), *a mountain hut.* 2. Gŭsh, *a rapid outflowing.* 3. Păt'terned, *marked off in figures or patterns.* 4. Lĭst, *hearken to.*

XXXII. CIRCUMSTANCES ALTER CASES.

1. *Derby.* Good morning, neighbor Scrapewell. I have half a dozen miles to ride to-day, and shall be extremely obliged if you will lend me your gray mare.

2. *Scrapewell.* It would give me great pleasure to oblige you, friend Derby; but I am under the necessity of going to the mill this very morning, with a bag of corn. My wife wants the meal to-day, and you know what a time there'll be if I disappoint her.

3. *D*. Then she must want it still, for I can assure you the mill does not go to-day. I heard the miller tell Will Davis that the water was too low.

4. *S*. You don't say so! That is bad, indeed; for in that case I shall be obliged to gallop off to town for the meal. My wife would comb my head for me if I should neglect it.

5. *D*. I can save you this journey, for I have plenty of meal at home, and will lend your wife as much as she wants.

6. *S*. Ah! neighbor Derby, I am sure your meal would never suit my wife. You can't conceive how whimsical she is.

7. *D*. If she were ten times more whimsical than she is, I am certain she would like it; for you sold it to me yourself, and you assured me it was the best you ever had.

8. *S*. Yes, yes! that's true, indeed; I always have the best of everything. You know, neighbor Derby, that no one is more ready to oblige a friend than I am; but I must tell you the mare this morning refused to eat hay; and, truly, I am afraid she will not carry you.

9. *D*. Oh, never fear! I will feed her well with oats on the road.

10. *S*. Oats! neighbor; oats are very dear.

11. *D*. Never mind that. When I have a good job in view, I never stand for trifles.

12. *S*. But it is very slippery; and I am really afraid she will fall and break your neck.

13. *D*. Give yourself no uneasiness about that. The mare is certainly sure-footed; and, besides, you were just now talking of galloping her to town.

14. *S*. Well, then, to tell you the plain truth,

though I wish to oblige you with all my heart, my saddle is torn quite in pieces, and I have just sent my bridle to be mended.

15. *D.* Luckily, I have both a bridle and a saddle hanging up at home.

16. *S.* Ah! that may be; but I am sure your saddle will never fit my mare. She's very notional.

17. *D.* Why, then I'll borrow neighbor Clodpole's.

18. *S.* Clodpole's! his will no more fit than yours.

19. *D.* At the worst, then, I will go to my good friend, Squire Jones. He has half a score of them; and I am sure he will lend me one that will fit her.

20. *S.* You know, friend Derby, that no one is more willing to oblige his neighbors than I am. I do assure you the beast should be at your service, with all my heart; but she has not been curried, I believe, for three weeks past. Her foretop and mane want combing and cutting very much. If any one should see her in her present plight, it would ruin the sale of her.

21. *D.* Oh, a horse is soon curried, and my son Sam shall attend to it at once.

22. *S.* Yes, very likely; but I this moment recollect the creature has no shoes on.

23. *D.* Well, is there not a blacksmith hard by?

24. *S.* What, that tinker, Dobson? I would not trust such a bungler to shoe a goat. No, no; none but uncle Tom Thumper shall shoe my mare.

25. *D.* As good luck will have it, then, I shall pass right by his door.

26. *S.* [*Calling to his son.*] Tim, Tim! here's neighbor Derby, who wants the loan of the gray mare, to ride to town to-day. You know the skin was

rubbed off her back, last week, a hand's breadth or more. [*Gives Tim a wink.*] However, I believe she is well enough by this time. You know, Tim, how ready I am to oblige my neighbors; indeed, we ought to do all the good we can in this world. We must certainly let neighbor Derby have her if she will possibly answer his purpose. Yes, yes; I see plainly by Tim's countenance, neighbor Derby, that he's disposed to oblige you. I would not have refused you

the mare for the worth of her. If I had, I should have expected you to refuse me in turn. None of my neighbors can accuse me of being backward in doing them a kindness whenever it is possible. Come, Tim, what do you say?

27. *Tim.* What do I say, father? Why, sir, I say that I am no less ready than you are to do a neighborly kindness. But the mare is by no means capable of performing the journey. About a hand's breadth, did you say? Why, sir, the skin is torn from the poor creature's back the bigness of your broad-brimmed hat! And, besides, I have promised her, so

soon as she is able to travel, to Ned Saunders, to carry a load of apples to market.

28. *S.* Do you hear that, neighbor? I am very sorry matters are thus. I would not have disobliged you for the price of two such mares. Believe me, neighbor Derby, I am really sorry, for your sake, that matters turn out thus.

29. *D.* And I as much for yours, neighbor Scrapewell; for to tell you the truth I received a letter this morning from Mr. Griffin, who tells me if I will be in town to-day he will give me the refusal of all that lot of timber, which he is about cutting down, on the side of the hill; and I had intended you should have shared half of it, which would have been not less than fitly dollars in your pocket. But, as your—

30. *S.* Fifty dollars, did you say?

31. *D.* Ay, truly, did I; but as your mare is out of order, I'll go and see if I can get old Roan, the blacksmith's horse.

32. *S.* Old Roan! My mare is at your service, neighbor, Here, Tim, tell Ned Saunders he can't have the mare: neighbor Derby wants her; and I won't refuse so good a friend anything he asks for.

33. *D.* But what are you to do for meal?

34. *S.* My wife can do without it for a week if you want the mare so long.

35. *D.* But, then, your saddle is all in pieces.

36. *S.* I meant the old one. I have bought a new one since, and you shall have the first use of it.

37. *D.* And shall I call at Thumper's and get the mare shod?

38. *S.* No, no; I had forgotten to tell you that I let neighbor Dobson shoe her, last week, by way

of trial; and, to do him justice, he shoes extremely well.

39. *D.* But, if the poor creature has lost so much skin from off her back—

40. *S.* Poh, poh! That is just one of Tim's large stories. I do assure you it was not, at first, bigger than my thumb nail, and I am certain it has not grown any since.

41. *D.* At least, however, let her have something she will eat, since she refuses hay.

42. *S.* She did, indeed, refuse hay this morning; but the only reason was that she was crammed full of oats. You have nothing to fear, neighbor; the mare is in perfect trim; and she will skim you over the ground like a bird. I wish you a good journey and a profitable job.

DEFINITIONS.—1. Ex-trēme'ly, *very much.* 6. Whĭm'şi-ᴄal, *full of whims.* 20. Cŭr'ried, *cleaned.* Fōre'tŏp, *hair on the forepart of the head.* 24. Bŭn̲'ḡler, *a clumsy workman.* 26. Dis-pōṣed', *inclined to.* Băck'ward, *slow, unwilling.* 27. Cä'pa-ble, *possessing ability.* Per-fôrm'ing, *accomplishing.* 29. Re-fūṣ'al, *choice of taking.* 42. Crămmed, *stuffed.*

XXXIII. THE NOBLEST REVENGE.

1. "I will have revenge on him, that I will, and make him heartily repent it," said Philip to himself, with a countenance quite red with anger. His mind was so engaged that he did not see Stephen, who happened at that instant to meet him.

2. "Who is that," said Stephen, "on whom you intend to be revenged?" Philip, as if awakened from a

dream, stopped short, and looking at his friend, soon resumed a smile that was natural to his countenance. "Ah," said he, "you remember my bamboo, a very pretty cane which was given me by my father, do you not? Look! there it is in pieces. It was farmer Robinson's son who reduced it to this worthless state."

3. Stephen very coolly asked him what had induced young Robinson to break it. "I was walking peaceably along," replied he, "and was playing with my cane by twisting it round my body. By accident, one of the ends slipped out of my hand, when I was opposite the gate, just by the wooden bridge, where the ill natured fellow had put down a pitcher of water, which he was taking home from the well."

4. "It so happened that my cane, in springing back, upset the pitcher, but did not break it. He came up close to me, and began to call me names, when I assured him that what I had done had happened by accident, and that I was sorry for it. Without regarding what I said, he instantly seized my cane, and twisted it, as you see; but I will make him repent of it."

5. "To be sure," said Stephen, "he is a very wicked boy, and is already very properly punished for being such, since nobody likes him or will have anything to do with him. He can scarcely find a companion to play with him; and is often at a loss for amusement, as he deserves to be. This, properly considered, I think will appear sufficient revenge for you."

6. "All this is true," replied Philip, "but he has broken my cane. It was a present from my father, and a very pretty cane it was. I offered to fill his

pitcher for him again, as I knocked it down by accident. I will be revenged."

7. "Now, Philip;" said Stephen, "I think you will act better in not minding him, as your contempt will be the best punishment you can inflict upon him. Be assured, he will always be able to do more mischief to you than you choose to do to him. And, now I think of it, I will tell you what happened to him not long since."

8. "Very unluckily for him, he chanced to see a bee hovering about a flower which he caught, and was going to pull off its wings out of sport, when the animal stung him, and flew away in safety to the hive. The pain put him into a furious passion, and, like you, he vowed revenge. He accordingly procured a stick, and thrust it into the beehive."

9. "In an instant the whole swarm flew out, and alighting upon him stung him in a hundred different places. He uttered the most piercing cries, and rolled upon the ground in the excess of his agony. His father immediately ran to him, but could not put the bees to flight until they had stung him so severely that he was confined several days to his bed."

10. "Thus, you see, he was not very successful in his pursuit of revenge. I would advise you, therefore, to pass over his insult. He is a wicked boy, and much stronger than you; so that your ability to obtain this revenge may be doubtful."

11. "I must own," replied Philip, "that your advice seems very good. So come along with me, and I will tell my father the whole matter, and I think he will not be angry with me." They went, and Philip told his father what had happened. He thanked Stephen for the good advice he had given his son,

and promised Philip to give him another cane exactly like the first.

12. A few days afterward, Philip saw this ill-natured boy fall as he was carrying home a heavy log of wood, which he could not lift up again. Philip ran to him, and helped him to replace it on his shoulder. Young Robinson was quite ashamed at the thought of this unmerited kindness, and heartily repented of his behavior. Philip went home quite satisfied. "This," said he, "is the noblest vengeance I could take, in returning good for evil. It is impossible I should repent of it."

DEFINITIONS.—l. Re-vĕnġe', *return for an injury.* Re-pĕnt', *to feel sorry for.* Coun'te-nançe, *the face.* 2. Re-ṣūmed', *took again.* 3. In-dūçed', *caused.* 4. As-ṣured', *declared positively.* Re-ġärd'ing, *noticing.* 5. Con-sĭd'ered, *thought of carefully.* 7. Con-tĕmpt', *disdain, scorn.* In-flĭet', *to impose, to put on.* 8. Hŏv'er-ing, *hanging over or about.* 9. Aġ'o-ny, *very great pain.* 10. A-bĭl'i-ty, *power.*

Exercises.—What is revenge? Is it right to take revenge on those who injure us? How should we treat such persons?

XXXIV. EVENING HYMN.

1. Come to the sunset tree,
        The day is past and gone;
    The woodman's ax lies free,
        And the reaper's work is done;
    The twilight star to heaven,
        And the summer dew to flowers,
    And rest to us is given,
        By the soft evening hours.

2. Sweet is the hour of rest,
    Pleasant the woods' low sigh,
And the gleaming of the west,
    And the turf whereon we lie,
When the burden and the heat
    Of the laborer's task is o'er,
And kindly voices greet
    The tired one at the door.

3. Yes, tuneful is the sound
    That dwells in whispering boughs:
Welcome the freshness round,
    And the gale that fans our brows;
But rest more sweet and still
    Than ever the nightfall gave,
Our yearning hearts shall fill,
    In the world beyond the grave.

4. There, shall no tempests blow,
    Nor scorching noontide heat;
There, shall be no more snow,
    No weary, wandering feet;
So we lift our trusting eyes
    From the hills our fathers trod,
To the quiet of the skies,
    To the Sabbath of our God.

XXXV. HOW MARGERY WONDERED.

By Lucy Larcom.

1. One bright morning late in March, little Margery put on her hood and her Highland plaid shawl, and went trudging across the beach. It was the first time she had been trusted out alone, for Margery was a little girl; nothing about her was large, except her round gray eyes, which had yet scarcely opened upon half a dozen springs and summers.

2. There was a pale mist on the far-off sea and sky, and up around the sun were white clouds edged with the hues of pinks and violets. The sunshine and the mild air made Margery's very heart feel warm, and she let the soft wind blow aside her Highland shawl, as she looked across the waters at the sun, and wondered! For, somehow, the sun had never looked before as it did to-day;—it seemed like a great golden flower bursting out of its pearl-lined calyx,—a flower without a stem. Or was there a strong stem away behind it in the sky, that reached down below the sea, to a root, nobody could guess where?

3. Margery did not stop to puzzle herself about the answer to her question, for now the tide, was coming in, and the waves, little at first, but growing larger every moment, were crowding up along the sand and pebbles, laughing, winking, and whispering, as they tumbled over each other, like thousands of children hurrying home from somewhere, each with its own precious little secret to tell.

4. Where did the waves come from? Who was down there under the blue wall of the horizon, with the hoarse, hollow voice, urging and pushing them

across the beach at her feet? And what secret was it they were lisping to each other with their pleasant voices? Oh, what was there beneath the sea, and beyond the sea, so deep, so broad, and so dim, too, away off where the white ships, that looked smaller than sea birds, were gliding out and in?

5. But while Margery stood still for a moment on a dry rock, and wondered, there came a low, rippling warble to her ear from a cedar tree on the cliff above her. It had been a long winter, and Margery had forgotten that there were birds, and that birds could sing. So she wondered again what the music was.

6. And when she saw the bird perched on a yellow-brown bough, she wondered yet more. It was only a bluebird, but then it was the first bluebird Margery had ever seen. He fluttered among the prickly twigs,

and looked as if he had grown out of them, as the cedar berries had, which were dusty blue, the color of his coat. But how did the music get in his throat? And after it was in his throat, how could it untangle itself, and wind itself off so evenly? And where had the bluebird flown from, across the snow banks down to the shore of the blue sea?

7. The waves sang a welcome to him, and he sang a welcome to the waves; they seemed to know each other well; and the ripple and the warble sounded so much alike, the bird and the wave must have both learned their music of the same teacher. And Margery kept on wondering as she stepped between the song of the bluebird and the echo of the sea, and climbed a sloping bank, just turning faintly green in the spring sunshine.

8. The grass was surely beginning to grow! There were fresh, juicy shoots running up among the withered blades of last year, as if in hopes of bringing them back to life; and closer down she saw the sharp points of new spears peeping from their sheaths. And scattered here and there were small, dark green leaves folded around buds shut up so tightly that only those who had watched them many seasons could tell what flowers were to be let out of their safe prisons by and by. So no one could blame Margery for not knowing that they were only common things, nor for stooping over the tiny buds, and wondering.

9. What made the grass come up so green out of the black earth? And how did the buds know when it was time to take off their little green hoods, and see what there was in the world around them? And how came they to be buds at all? Did they bloom in another world before they sprung up here?—and did

they know, themselves, what kind of flowers they should blossom into? Had flowers souls, like little girls, that would live in another world when their forms had faded away in this?

10. Margery thought she would like to sit down on the bank, and wait beside the buds until they opened; perhaps they would tell her their secret if the very first thing they saw was her eyes watching them. One bud was beginning to unfold; it was streaked with yellow in little stripes that she could imagine became wider every minute. But she would not touch it, for it seemed almost as much alive as herself. She only wondered, and wondered!

11. Margery heard her mother calling her, and she trudged home across the shells and pebbles with a pleasant smile dimpling her cheeks; for she felt very much at home in this large, wonderful world, and was happy to be alive, although she neither could have told, nor cared to know, the reason why. But when her mother unpinned the little girl's Highland shawl, and took off her hood, she said, "O mother, do let me live on the doorstep! I don't like houses to stay in. What makes everything so pretty and so glad? Don't you like to wonder?"

12. Margery's mother was a good woman. But then there was all the housework to do, and, if she had thoughts, she did not often let them wander outside of the kitchen door. And just now she was baking some gingerbread, which was in danger of getting burned in the oven. So she pinned the shawl around the child's neck again, and left her on the doorstep, saying to herself, as she returned to her work, "Queer child! I wonder what kind of a woman she will be!"

13. But Margery sat on the doorstep, and wondered, as the sea sounded louder, and the sunshine grew warmer around her. It was all so strange, and grand, and beautiful! Her heart danced with joy to the music that went echoing through the wide world from the roots of the sprouting grass to the great golden blossom of the sun.

14. And when the round, gray eyes closed that night, at the first peep of the stars, the angels looked down and wondered over Margery. For the wisdom of the wisest being God has made, ends in wonder; and there is nothing on earth so wonderful as the budding soul of a little child.

DEFINITIONS.-1. Trūdğ'ing, *walking sturdily.* 2. Hūeṣ, *colors.* Cā'lyx, *the outer covering of a flower.* 4. Ho-rī'zon, *the line where the sky and earth seem to meet.* 5. War̤'ble, *a trill of the voice.* Spēarṣ, shoots of grass. Shēaths, *coverings.*

Exercises.—Name the things about which Margery wondered. What did she wonder about each? What is still more wonderful than all that at which Margery wondered?

XXXVI. THE CHILD'S WORLD.

1. "Great, wide, beautiful, wonderful world,
    With the wonderful water round you curled,
    And the wonderful grass upon your breast,—
    World, you are beautifully drest."

2. "The wonderful air is over me,
    And the wonderful wind is shaking the tree;
    It walks on the water, and whirls the mills,
    And talks to itself on the tops of the hills."

3. "You friendly Earth! how far do you go
  With the wheat fields that nod, and the rivers
      that flow;
  With cities and gardens, and cliffs and isles,
  And people upon you for thousands of miles?"

4. "Ah, you are so great, and I am so small,
  I tremble to think of you, World, at all:
  And yet, when I said my prayers, to-day,
  A whisper inside me seemed to say,
  You are more than the Earth, though you are
      such a dot:
  You can love and think, and the Earth can
      not!'"

XXXVII. SUSIE'S COMPOSITION.

1. Susie Smith came home from school one day, and had no sooner entered the sitting room than she burst into tears. "What is the matter, my dear child?" said her mother, drawing her daughter to her side and smiling.

2. "O mother, matter enough," sobbed Susie. "All our class must bring in compositions to-morrow morning, and I never, never can write one. We must write twelve lines at least, and I have written only a few words after trying nearly all the afternoon. See what work I have made of it!"

3. Mrs. Smith took the rumpled, tear-stained paper which Susie held in her hand, and glanced at what she had written. In a careful hand she had tried to

write upon three themes: "Time," "Temperance," and "Industry."

4. "Time is short. We should all improve our time." "Temperance is a very useful thing." "We should all be industrious if we wish to do anything in the world." These sentences were all she had written.

5. "Now," said Susie, "I can't think of another word to say upon any of these subjects, and I know I shall have to go to school without a composition, for I won't be so mean as to copy one from a book, or to ask you or papa to write one for me."

6. "That is right, my dear," said her mother. "You will be far happier with a poor composition, if it is all your own, than with a fine one written by somebody else. But cheer up. You have not begun right—you have been trying to write upon subjects that you know nothing about. Run into the garden and play. I will call you in half an hour."

7. "But my composition," began Susie. "Don't think about your composition while you are gone," said Mrs. Smith, "but have as pleasant a time as you can."

8. It seemed but a few minutes to Susie before she heard her mother's voice calling her. She went into the house at once—her hands full of sweet flowers, and her cheeks rosy with exercise.

9. "Now, Susie," said her mother, "I want you to sit by the window with this nice sheet of paper and a pencil, and write something about what you can see." "But my composition, mother," said Susie; "when shall I begin that?" "Never mind your composition, my dear; do this to please me, and we will talk about that by and by."

10. Susie thought her mother's request was a strange one; but she knew that she always had a good reason for everything she did: so she took the paper and pencil, and sat by the window.

11. "Do not talk to me at all," said her mother. "Look out of the window, and then write down your thoughts about everything you see."

12. Susie could not help laughing, it seemed such a funny thing to be doing. As she looked out, she first saw the western sky and some bright, sunset clouds. "O mother!" she exclaimed, "what a splendid sunset!" "Don't talk," said her mother, "but write."

13. "I'll write about the sunset, then," said she, and the pencil began to move rapidly across the paper. In a few moments she said, "Mother, shall I read you what I have written?" "No, not now," answered her mother; "I am going into the dining room. You may sit and write until I return."

14. As Susie went on writing, she became very much interested in her occupation, and for a time forgot all about the dreaded composition. She wrote about the sunset clouds, the appearance of the distant hills, the trees, the river, the garden with its gay flowers, and the birds flying past the window.

15. Just as she had reached the bottom of the page, her mother came in. "Well, Susie," said she, with a smile, "how does that composition come on?" "Composition!" exclaimed Susie; "you told me not to think about my composition, and I have not thought of it once; I have had such a nice time writing about what I could see from the window."

16. Mrs. Smith took the paper and read aloud what Susie had written: "I am sitting on a low seat at the bay window, one half of which is open, so that I can

smell the sweet flowers in the garden. The sky is all bright with sunset; I can see purple, and pink, and golden. I do not believe that anyone on earth has a paint box with such lovely colors in it."

17. "I can see one cloud, far above the rest, that looks like a ship sailing in the blue sea. I should like to sail on a cloud, if it would not make me dizzy. Now, while I have been writing, the clouds have changed in color and form, but they are just as beautiful as they were before."

18. "The green hills are tipped with light, and look as if they were wearing golden crowns. I can see a river a great way off, and it looks quite still, although I know it is running as fast as it can to get to the ocean."

19. "The birds are flying past the window to go home and take care of their little ones. I am glad the birds are not afraid to live in our garden, and to build nests in our trees."

20. "Our garden is full of flowers—pinks, lilies, and roses. Mother calls this the month of roses. My birthday will come in a week, and we can have all the flowers we wish for wreaths and bouquets."

21. "There, Susie," said Mrs. Smith, "that is a very nice composition, indeed." "A composition!" exclaimed Susie, "is that a composition?" "Yes, my dear, and a very good one, too," replied her mother. "When it hasn't even a subject?"

22. "We can find one for it, and I do not doubt it will please your teacher, as it does me. You see, my dear," continued her mother, "that it is easy enough to write if you have anything interesting to write about."

23. The next morning Susie copied her composition very neatly, and started to school with a happy heart, saying, as she gave her mother a kiss, "Just think how funny it is, dear mother, that I should have written so long a composition without knowing it."

DEFINITIONS.—Cŏm-po-ṣĭ'tion, *that which is thought out and arranged, a written or literary work.* 3. Rŭm'pled, *wrinkled, creased.* Thēmeṣ, *subjects or topics on which a person writes.* 10. Re-quĕst', *that which is asked.* 14. Oc-cu-pā'tion, *that which employs the time.* 20. Bọu-quets' (*pro.* bōō-kāṣ'), *bunches of flowers.*

EXERCISES.—What is a composition? Why was Susie so troubled? Why could she not write about "Time," "Temperance," or "Industry"? What did her mother have her do? What did Susie write? Was it a composition? Did she know, at the time, that it was? What fault did she find with it? Can you give her composition a proper subject?

XXXVIII. THE SUMMER SHOWER.

The author, **Thomas Buchanan Read**, was born in Chester Co., Pa., March 12, 1822. His life was devoted to the fine arts, and he attained a high reputation both as artist and poet. He died in New York, May 11, 1872.

1. Before the stout harvesters falleth the grain,
   As when the strong storm-wind is reaping the plain,
   And loiters the boy in the briery lane;
   But yonder aslant comes the silvery rain,
Like a long line of spears brightly burnished and tall.

2. Adown the white highway like cavalry fleet,
   It dashes the dust with its numberless feet.
   Like a murmurless school, in their leafy retreat,
   The wild birds sit listening the drops round them
      beat;
And the boy crouches close to the blackberry wall.

3. The swallows alone take the storm on the wing,
   And, taunting the tree-sheltered laborers, sing.
   Like pebbles the rain breaks the face of the spring,
   While a bubble darts up from each widening ring;
And the boy in dismay hears the loud shower fall.

4. But soon are the harvesters tossing their sheaves;
   The robin darts out from his bower of leaves;
   The wren peereth forth from the moss-covered
      eaves;
   And the rain-spattered urchin now gladly perceives
That the beautiful bow bendeth over them all.

Definitions.—1. A-slant′, *toward one side*. 2. High′way, *a public road.* Re-treat′, *a place of refuge or safety.* Crouch′es, *stoops low.* 3. Taunt′ing, *deriding, mocking.* 4. Ur′chin, *a child.*

XXXIX. CONSEQUENCES OF IDLENESS.

1. Many young persons seem to think it of not much consequence if they do not improve their time well in youth, vainly expecting that they can make it up by diligence when they are older. They also think it is disgraceful for men and women to be idle, but that there can be no harm for persons who are young to spend their time in any manner they please.

2. George Jones thought so. When he was twelve years old, he went to an academy to prepare to enter college. His father was at great expense in obtaining books for him, clothing him, and paying his tuition. But George was idle. The preceptor of the academy would often tell him that if he did not study diligently when young he would never succeed well.

3. But George thought of nothing but present pleasure. He would often go to school without having made any preparation for his morning lesson; and, when called to recite with his class, he would stammer and make such blunders that the rest of the class could not help laughing at him. He was one of the poorest scholars in the school, because he was one of the most idle.

4. When recess came, and all the boys ran out of the academy upon the playground, idle George would come moping along. Instead of studying diligently while in school, he was indolent and half asleep. When the proper time for play came, he had no relish for it. I recollect very well, that, when "tossing up" for a game of ball, we used to choose everybody on the playground before we chose George;

and if there were enough without him we used to leave him out. Thus he was unhappy in school and out of school.

5. There is nothing which makes a person enjoy play so well as to study hard. When recess was over, and the rest of the boys returned, fresh and vigorous, to their studies, George might be seen lagging and moping along to his seat. Sometimes he would be asleep in school; sometimes he would pass his time in catching flies, and penning them up in little holes, which he cut in his seat; and sometimes, when the preceptor's back was turned, he would throw a paper ball across the room.

6. When the class was called up to recite, George would come drowsily along, looking as mean and ashamed as though he were going to be whipped. The rest of the class stepped up to the recitation with alacrity, and appeared happy and contented. When it came George's turn to recite, he would be so long in doing it, and make such blunders, that all most heartily wished him out of the class.

7. At last, George went with his class to enter college. Though he passed a very poor examination, he was admitted with the rest; for those who examined him thought it was possible that the reason why he did not answer questions better was because he was frightened. Now came hard times for poor George. In college there is not much mercy shown to bad scholars; and George had neglected his studies so long that he could not now keep up with his class, let him try ever so hard.

8. He could, without much difficulty, get along in the academy, where there were only two or three boys of his own class to laugh at him. But now he had

to go into a large recitation room, filled with students from all parts of the country. In the presence of all these, he must rise and recite to a professor. Poor fellow! He paid dearly for his idleness.

9. You would have pitied him if you could have seen him trembling in his scat, every moment expecting to be called upon to recite. And when he was called upon, he would stand up and take what the class called a "dead set;" that is, he could not recite at all. Sometimes he would make such ludicrous blunders that the whole class would burst into a laugh. Such are the applauses an idler gets. He was wretched, of course. He had been idle so long that he hardly knew how to apply his mind to study. All the good scholars avoided him; they were ashamed to be seen in his company. He became discouraged, and gradually grew dissipated.

10. The officers of the college were soon compelled to suspend him. He returned in a few months, but did no better; and his father was then advised to take him from college. He left college, despised by everyone. A few months ago, I met him, a poor wanderer, without money and without friends. Such are the wages of idleness. I hope every reader will, from this history, take warning, and "stamp improvement on the wings of time."

DEFINITIONS.—1. Cŏn´se-quençe, *importance*, *influence*. 2. A-ĕăd´e-my, *a school of high order*. Cŏl´leġe, *a seminary of learning of the highest order*. Pre-çĕp´tor, *a teacher*. 3. Prĕp-a-rā´-tion, *a making ready*. 5. Vĭg´or-oŭs, *full of activity and strength*. 6. A-lăc´ri-ty, *cheerfulness, sprightliness*. 8. Pro-fĕss´or, *a teacher in a college*. 9. Lū´di-crous, *adapted to raise laughter*. Ap-plaus´es, *praises*. Dĭs´-si-pāt-ed, *given up to bad habits*. 10. Im-prove´ment, *increase of knowledge*.

XL. ADVANTAGES OF INDUSTRY.

1. I gave you, in the last lesson, the history of George Jones, an idle boy, and showed you the consequences of his idleness. I shall now give you the history of Charles Bullard, a classmate of George. Charles was about the same age as George, and did not possess superior talents. Indeed, I doubt whether he was equal to him in natural powers of mind.

2. But Charles was a hard student. When quite young, he was always careful and diligent in school. Sometimes, when there was a very hard lesson, instead of going out to play during recess, he would stay in to study. He had resolved that his first object should be to get his lessons well, and then he could play with a good conscience. He loved play as well as any body, and was one of the best players on the ground. I hardly ever saw any boy catch a ball better than he could. When playing any game, everyone was glad to get Charles on his side.

3. I have said that Charles would sometimes stay in at recess. This, however, was very seldom; it was only when the lessons were very hard indeed. Generally, he was among the first on the playground, and he was also among the first to go into school when called. Hard study gave him a relish for play, and play again gave him a relish for hard study; so he was happy both in school and out. The preceptor could not help liking him, for he always had his lessons well committed, and never gave him any trouble.

4. When he went to enter college, the preceptor gave him a good recommendation. He was able to

answer all the questions which were put to him when he was examined. He had studied so well when he was in the academy, and was so thoroughly prepared for college, that he found it very easy to keep up with his class, and had much time for reading interesting books.

5. But he would always get his lesson well before he did anything else, and would review it just before recitation. When called upon to recite, he rose tranquil and happy, and very seldom made mistakes. The officers of the college had a high opinion of him, and he was respected by all the students.

6. There was, in the college, a society made up of all the best scholars. Charles was chosen a member of that society. It was the custom to choose some one of the society to deliver a public address every year. This honor was conferred on Charles; and he had studied so diligently, and read so much, that he delivered an address which was very interesting to all who heard it.

7. At last he graduated, as it is called; that is, he finished his collegiate course, and received his degree. It was known by all that he was a good scholar, and by all that he was respected. His father and mother, brothers and sisters, came on the commencement day to hear him speak.

8. They all felt gratified, and loved Charles more than ever. Many situations of usefulness and profit were opened to him; for Charles was now an intelligent man, and universally respected. He is still a useful and a happy man. He has a cheerful home, and is esteemed by all who know him.

9. Such are the rewards of industry. How strange it is that any person should be willing to live in idle-

ness when it will certainly make him unhappy! The idle boy is almost invariably poor and miserable; the industrious boy is happy and prosperous.

10. But perhaps some child who reads this, asks, "Does God notice little children in school?" He certainly does. And if you are not diligent in the improvement of your time, it is one of the surest evidences that your heart is not right with God. You are placed in this world to improve your time. In youth you must be preparing for future usefulness. And if you do not improve the advantages you enjoy, you sin against your Maker.

> With books, or work, or healthful play,
> Let your first years be passed;
> That you may give, for every day,
> Some good account, at last.

DEFINITIONS.—1. Hĭs'to-ry, *a description or a narration of events.* 2. Cŏn'sciençe, *our own knowledge of right and wrong.* Game, *play, sport.* 3. Com-mĭt'ted, *fixed in mind.* 4. Rĕc-ommen-dā'tion, *what is said in praise of anyone.* 5. Re-view', *to examine again.* Trăn'quil, *quiet, calm.* 6. Con-fĕrred', *given to or bestowed upon anyone.* 7. Grăd'ū-ā-ted, *received a degree from a college.* Com-mĕnçe'ment, *the day when students receive their degree.* 8. U-ni-vĕr'sal-ly, *by all, without exception.* 9. In-vā'ri-a-bly, *always, uniformly.* 10. Ev'i-den-çes, *proofs.* Ad-van'ta-ġes, *opportunities for improvement.*

Exercises.—What was the character of George Jones? Of Charles Bullard? How did George appear in the class at school? How did he behave at recess? How did Charles differ from him in these respects? Relate what happened when George went to college. What became of him? Did Charles succeed at college? Which of them do you think more worthy of imitation? What is said of the idle? What is said of the industrious? Who watches all our actions wherever we may be? For what are we placed in this world? Should you not then be diligent in your studies?

XLI. THE FOUNTAIN.

By **James Russell Lowell**, one of the most noted of American poets; also well known as an essayist and lecturer. He was born at Cambridge, Mass., in 1819, and died there in 1891.

1.

Into the sunshine,
    Full of the light,
Leaping and flashing,
    From morn till night!

2.

Into the moonlight,
    Whiter than snow,
Waving so flower-like
    When the winds blow!

3.

Into the starlight,
    Rushing in spray,
Happy at midnight,
    Happy by day!

4.

Ever in motion,
    Blithesome and cheery,
Still climbing heavenward,
    Never aweary;

5.

Glad of all weathers,
    Still seeming best,
Upward or downward,
    Motion, thy rest;

6.

Full of a nature
    Nothing can tame,
Changed every moment,
    Ever the same;

7.

Ceaseless aspiring,
    Ceaseless content,
Darkness or sunshine
    Thy element;

8.

Glorious fountain!
    Let my heart be
Fresh, changeful, constant,
    Upward like thee!

DEFINITIONS.—4. Blīthe′sòme, *gay.* Cheer′y, *in good spirits.* A-wēa′ry, *weary, tired.* 7. As-pīr′ing, *ambitious.* El′e-ment, *the proper habitation or sphere of anything, suitable state.* 8. Cŏn′-stant, *fixed, not to be changed.*

XLII. COFFEE.

1. The coffee tree is a native of eastern Africa, but it was in Arabia that it first became known to the people of Europe, and until about the year 1700 A. D. that country afforded the entire supply.

2. Then the coffee seeds found their way to Java, by means of some traders, and one of the first plants grown on that island was sent as a present to the governor of the Dutch East India Company, who lived in Holland.

3. It was planted in the Botanical Gardens at Amsterdam, and in a few years seeds taken from it were sent to South America, where the cultivation of coffee has steadily increased, extending to the West Indies, until now the offspring of this one plant produce more coffee than is obtained from all the other plants in the world.

4. The plant is an evergreen, and is from six to twelve feet high, the stem being from ten to fifteen inches in diameter. The lower branches bend down when the tree begins to grow old, and extend themselves into a round form somewhat like an umbrella; and the wood is so pliable that the ends of the largest branches may be bent down to within two or three feet of the earth.

5. The bark is whitish and somewhat rough. A tree is never without leaves, which are at small distances from one another, and on almost opposite sides of a bough. Blossoms and green and ripe fruit may be seen on the same tree at the same time. When the blossom falls off, there grows in its place a small green fruit, which becomes dark red as it ripens.

6. This fruit is not unlike a cherry, and is very good to eat. Under the pulp of this cherry is found the bean or berry we call coffee, wrapped in a fine, thin skin. The berry is at first very soft, and has a bad taste; but as the cherry ripens the berry grows harder, and the dried-up fruit becomes a shell or pod of a deep brown color.

7. The berry is now solid, and its color is a translucent green. Each shell contains two seeds, rounded on one side and flat on the other. The seeds lie with the flat sides together, and, in one highly prized variety, the two seeds grow together, forming one: this is known as the pea berry. When the fruit is so ripe that it can be shaken from the tree, the husks are separated from the berries, and are used, in Arabia, by the natives, while the berries are sold.

8. The young plants are inserted in holes from twelve to eighteen inches deep, and six or eight feet apart. If left to themselves, they would grow to the

height of eighteen or twenty feet; but they are usually dwarfed by pruning, so that the fruit may be easily got at by the gatherer.

9. Thus dwarfed, they extend their branches until they cover the whole space about them. They begin to yield fruit the third year. By the sixth or seventh year they are at full bearing, and continue to bear for twenty years or more.

10. Before the berry can be used, it undergoes a process of roasting. The amount of aromatic oil brought out in roasting has much to do with the market value of coffee, and it has been found that the longer the raw coffee is kept, the richer it becomes in this peculiar oil, and so the more valuable. But after the coffee is roasted, and especially after it is ground, it loses its aroma rapidly.

11. Arabia produces the celebrated Mocha, or "Mokha," coffee, which is the finest in the world; but little or none of the best product is ever taken out of that country. The Java coffee from the East Indies is next prized, but the best quality of this kind is also quite difficult to obtain, and many, therefore, prefer the finest grades of Rio coffee from South America to such Mocha and Java as can be had in our country.

DEFINITIONS.—1. Af-fōrd′ed, *yielded, produced.* 3. Off′sprĭng, *descendants, however remote, from, the stock.* 4. Plī′a-ble, *easily bent.* 7. Trans-lū′çent, *permitting the passage of light.* 8. Prŭn′-ing, *trimming.* 10. Ar-o-măt′ic, *containing aroma, fragrant.*

Exercises.—What country first supplied coffee? How did the plant come to be grown in other countries? Describe the plant. What is said of the fruit? How are the plants cultivated? What is said about the roasting of coffee? What are the three principal kinds of coffee used, and how are they valued?

XLIII. THE WINTER KING

1. Oh! what will become of thee, poor little bird?
   The muttering storm in the distance is heard;
   The rough winds are waking, the clouds growing
      black,
   They'll soon scatter snowflakes all over thy back!
   From what sunny clime hast thou wandered away?
   And what art thou doing this cold winter day?

2. "I'm picking the gum from the old peach tree;
   The storm doesn't trouble me. Pee, dee, dee!"

3. But what makes thee seem so unconscious of care?
   The brown earth is frozen, the branches are bare:
   And how canst thou be so light-hearted and free,
   As if danger and suffering thou never should'st see,
   When no place is near for thy evening nest,
   No leaf for thy screen, for thy bosom no rest?

4. "Because the same Hand is a shelter for me,
   That took off the summer leaves. Pee, dee, dee!"

5. But man feels a burden of care and of grief,
   While plucking the cluster and binding the sheaf:
   In the summer we faint, in the winter we're chilled,
   With ever a void that is yet to be filled.
   We take from the ocean, the earth, and the air,
   Yet all their rich gifts do not silence our care.

6. "A very small portion sufficient will be,
   If sweetened with gratitude. Pee, dee, dee!"

7. But soon there'll be ice weighing down the light
    bough,
On which thou art flitting so playfully now;
And though there's a vesture well fitted and warm,
Protecting the rest of thy delicate form,
What, then, wilt thou do with thy little bare feet,
To save them from pain, mid the frost and the sleet?

8. "I can draw them right up in my feathers, you see,
    To warm them, and fly away. Pee, dee, dee!"

9. I thank thee, bright monitor; what thou hast taught
Will oft be the theme of the happiest thought;
We look at the clouds; while the birds have an eye
To Him who reigns over them, changeless and high.
And now little hero, just tell me thy name,
That I may be sure whence my oracle came.

10. "Because, in all weather, I'm merry and free,
    They call me the Winter King. Pee, dee, dee!"

DEFINITIONS.—1. Mŭ′ter-ing, *murmuring, rumbling.* 3. Un-cŏn′scioŭs, *not knowing, not perceiving.* 5. Clŭs′ter, *a bunch.* 7. Flĭt′ing, *moving about in a lively manner.* Vĕst′ūre, *clothing, covering.* 9. Mŏn′i-tor, *one who warns of faults.* Or′a-ele, *a wise sentence or decision.*

XLIV. THE NETTLE.

1. *Anna.* O papa! I have stung my hand with that nettle.

2. *Father.* Well, my dear, I am sorry for it; but pull up that large dock leaf you see near it; now bruise the juice out of it on the part which is stung. Well, is the pain lessened?

3. *A.* Oh, very much indeed, I hardly feel it now. But I wish there was not a nettle in the world. I am sure I do not know what use there can be in them.

4. *F.* If you knew anything of botany, Nanny, you would not say so.

5. *A.* What is botany, papa?

6. *F.* Botany, my dear, is the knowledge of plants.

7. *A.* Some plants are very beautiful. If the lily were growing in our fields, I should not complain. But this ugly nettle! I do not know what beauty or use there can be in that.

8. *F.* And yet, Nanny, there is more beauty, use, and instruction in a nettle, than even in a lily.

9. *A.* O papa, how can you make that out?

10. *F.* Put on your gloves, pluck up that nettle, and let us examine it. First, look at the flower.

11. *A.* The flower, papa? I see no flower, unless those little ragged knobs are flowers, which have neither color nor smell, and are not much larger than the heads of pins.

12. *F.* Here, take this magnifying glass and examine them.

13. *A.* Oh, I see now; every little knob is folded up in leaves, like a rosebud. Perhaps there is a flower inside.

14. *F.* Try; take this pin and touch the knob. Well, what do you see?

15. *A.* Oh, how curious!

16. *F.* What is curious?

17. *A.* The moment I touched it, it flew open. A little cloud rose out like enchantment, and four beautiful little stems sprung up as if they were alive; and, now that I look again with the glass, I see an elegant little flower as nice and perfect as a lily itself.

18. F. Well, now examine the leaves.

19. A. Oh, I see they are all covered over with little bristles; and when I examine them with the glass, I see a little bag, filled with a juice like water, at the bottom of each. Ha! these are the things which stung me.

20. F. Now touch the little bag with the point of the pin.

21. A. When I press the bag, the juice runs up and comes out at the small point at the top; so I suppose the little thorn must be hollow inside, though it is finer than the point of my cambric needle.

22. F. Have all the leaves those stings?

23. A. No, papa; some of the young ones are quite green and soft, like velvet, and I may handle them without any danger.

24. F. Now look at the stem, and break it.

25. A. I can easily crack it, but I can not break it asunder, for the bark is so strong that it holds it together.

26. F. Well, now you see there are more curious things in the nettle than you expected.

27. A. Yes, indeed, I see that. But you have often told me that God makes nothing without its use; and I am sure I can not see any use in all these things.

28. F. That we will now consider. You saw the little flower burst open, and a cloud rose, you say, like enchantment. Now all this is necessary for the nature of the plant. There are many thousand plants in the world, and it has pleased God, in his wisdom, to make them all different. Now look at this other nettle, which grew on the opposite side of the road; you see that it is not exactly like the one you have just examined.

29. A. No, papa; this has little flat seeds instead of flowers.

30. F. Very right, my dear. Now, in order to make those seeds grow, it is necessary that the little flower of this plant and the seed of that should be together, as they are in most others. But plants can not walk, like animals. The wisdom of God, therefore, has provided a remedy for this. When the little flower bursts open it throws out a fine powder, which you saw rise like a cloud; this is conveyed by the air to the other plant, and when it falls upon the seed of that plant it gives it power to grow, and makes it a perfect seed, which, in its turn, when it falls to the ground, will produce a new plant. Were it not for this fine powder, that seed would never be perfect or complete.

31. A. That is very curious, indeed; and I see the use of the little cloud and the flower; but the leaf that stung me, of what use can that be? There, dear papa, I am afraid I puzzle you to tell me that.

32. P. Even these stings are made useful to man. The poor people in some countries use them instead of blisters, when they are sick. Those leaves which do not sting are used by some for food, and from the stalk others get a stringy bark, which answers the purpose of flax. Thus you see that even the despised nettle is not made in vain; and this lesson may serve to teach you that we only need to understand the works of God to see that "in goodness and wisdom he has made them all."

DEFINITIONS.—12. Măḡ′ni-fȳ-ing-ḡlȧss, *an instrument used to make objects appear larger.* 17. En-chȧnt′ment, *magic art, witch-craft.* 5. A-sŭn′der, *apart, into parts.* 30. Rĕm′e-dy, *that which removes an evil.* Con-vẹyed′, *carried.* 32. Strĭng′y, *full of strings.*

XLV. THE TEMPEST.

By **James T. Fields** (born 1817, died 1881), who was born at Portsmouth, N. H. He was a poet, and the author, also, of some well known prose works. Of these, his "Yesterdays with Authors" is the most noted.

1. We were crowded in the cabin;
    Not a soul would dare to sleep:
   It was midnight on the waters,
    And a storm was on the deep.

2. 'T is a fearful thing in winter
    To be shattered by the blast,
   And to hear the rattling trumpet
    Thunder, "Cut away the mast!"

3. So we shuddered there in silence,
    For the stoutest held his breath,
   While the hungry sea was roaring,
    And the breakers threatened death.

4. And as thus we sat in darkness,
    Each one busy in his prayers,
   "We are lost!" the captain shouted,
    As he staggered down the stairs.

5. But his little daughter whispered,
    As she took his icy hand,
   "Is n't God upon the ocean,
    Just the same as on the land?"

6. Then we kissed the little maiden,
    And we spoke in better cheer;
   And we anchored safe in harbor
    When the morn was shining clear.

DEFINITIONS.—1. Deep, *the ocean.* 2. Blàst, *tempest.* 3. Breāk'ers, *waves of the sea broken by rocks.* 6. Cheer, *state of mind.*

XLVI. THE CREATOR.

The poetry at the close of this selection is by **John Keble**, a celebrated English clergyman, born in 1792. He held for some years the professorship of Poetry at Oxford University.

1. Come, and I will show you what is beautiful. It is a rose fully blown. See how she sits upon her mossy stem, the queen of flowers. Her leaves glow like fire. The air is filled with her sweet odor. She is the delight of every eye.

2. But there is one fairer than the rose. He that made the rose is more beautiful than the rose. He is altogether lovely. He is the delight of every heart.

3. I will show you what is strong. The lion is strong. When he raiseth himself up from his lair, when he shaketh his mane, when the voice of his roaring is heard, the cattle of the field fly, and the wild beasts of the desert hide themselves; for he is terrible.

4. But He who made the lion is stronger than the lion. He can do all things. He gave us life, and in a moment can take it away, and no one can save us from his hand.

5. I will show you what is glorious. The sun is glorious. When he shineth in the clear sky, when he sitteth on his throne in the heavens, and looketh abroad over the earth, he is the most glorious and excellent object the eye can behold.

6. But He who made the sun is more glorious than the sun. The eye cannot look on his dazzling brightness. He seeth all dark places, by night as well as by day. The light of his countenance is over all the world.

7. This great Being is God. He made all things, but He is more excellent than all that He has made. He is the Creator, they are the creatures. They may be beautiful, but He is Beauty. They may be strong, but He is Strength. They may be perfect, but He is Perfection.

8. There is a book, who runs may read,
   Which heavenly truth imparts,
   And all the lore its scholars need—
   Pure eyes and loving hearts.

9. The works of God, above, below,
   Within us, and around,
   Are pages in that book, to show
   How God himself is found.

10. The glorious sky, embracing all,
    Is like the Father's love;
    Wherewith encompassed, great and small
    In peace and order move.

11. Thou who hast given me eyes to see
    And love this sight so fair,
    Give me a heart to find out Thee
    And read Thee everywhere.

DEFINITIONS.—1. Blōwn, *blossomed, bloomed.* O'dor, *smell, scent.* 3. Lâir, *bed of a wild beast.* Dĕş'ert, *a wilderness, a place where no one lives.* 5. Ex'çel-lent, *surpassing others in worth, superior.* 6. Dăz'zling, *overpowering with light.* 7. Per-fĕc'tion, *the state of being perfect, so that nothing is wanting.* 8. Im-pärts', *makes known.* Lōre, *learning.* 10. En-cŏm'passed, *surrounded.*

Exercises.—What is described as beautiful? As strong? As glorious? Who is more beautiful than the rose, stronger than the lion, and more glorious than the sun? What is the book which we may all read? What should it teach us?

XLVII. THE HORSE.

1. Uncle Thomas. Well, boys, I am glad to see you again. Since I last saw you I have made quite a tour, and at some future time will describe to you what I have seen. I promised at this meeting, however, to tell you something about animals, and I propose to begin with the horse. But I know that you like stories better than lecturing, so I will proceed at once to tell you some which I have gathered for you.

2. Frank. We never feel tired of listening to you, Uncle Thomas. We know you always have something curious to tell us.

3. Uncle Thomas. Well then, Frank, to begin at once with the horse.

4. In several parts of the world there are to be found large herds of wild horses. In South America the immense plains are inhabited by them, and it is said that ten thousand are sometimes found in a single herd. These herds are always preceded by a leader, who directs their motions; and such is the regularity with which they perform their movements, that it seems as if they could hardly be surpassed by the best trained cavalry.

5. It is extremely dangerous for travelers to meet a herd of this description. When they are unaccustomed to the sight of such a mass of creatures, they can not help feeling greatly alarmed at their rapid and apparently irresistible approach. The trampling of the animals sounds like distant thunder; and such is the rapidity and impetuosity of their advance, that it seems to threaten instant destruction.

6. Sometimes, however, they suddenly stop short, utter a loud and piercing neigh, and, with a rapid wheel, take an opposite course, and altogether disappear. On such occasions it requires great care in the traveler to prevent his horses from breaking loose and escaping with the wild herd.

7. In those countries where wild horses are so plentiful, the inhabitants do not take the trouble to raise others, but whenever they want one they mount upon an animal accustomed to the sport, and gallop over the plain toward a herd, which is readily found at no great distance.

8. The rider gradually approaches some stragglers from the main body, and, having selected the one he wishes, he dexterously throws the lasso (which is a

long rope with a running noose, and is firmly fixed to his saddle) either over the wild horse's head or in such a manner as to entangle his hind legs; and by the sudden checking of his own horse, he throws the captured animal over on its side.

9. In an instant he jumps off his horse, wraps his cloak round the head of the captive, forces a bit into his mouth, and straps a saddle on his back. He then removes the cloak, and the animal starts to his feet. With equal quickness the hunter leaps into his saddle; and, in spite of the kicking of the captive, keeps his seat, till, being wearied out with his efforts, the horse submits to the guidance of his new master, and is reduced to complete obedience.

10. Frank. But, Uncle Thomas, are all horses originally wild? I have heard that Arabia is famous for raising horses.

11. Uncle Thomas. Arabia has, for a long time, been noted for the beauty and speed of its horses. It is not strange, however, that the Arabian horse should be the most excellent, when we consider the care and kindness with which it is treated. One of the best stories which I have ever heard of the love of an Arabian for his steed, is that related of an Arab, from whom an English officer wished to purchase his horse.

12. The animal was a bright bay mare, of fine form and great beauty; and the owner, proud of her appearance and qualities, paraded her before the Englishman's tent until she attracted his attention. On being asked if he would sell her, "What will you give me?" was the reply. "That depends upon her age. I suppose she is past five?" "Guess again," said he. "Four?" "Look at her mouth," said the Arab, with

a smile. On examination she was found to be about three. This, from her size and symmetry, greatly increased her value.

13. The gentleman said, "I will give you eighty tomans," (nearly two hundred and fifty dollars). "A little more, if you please," said the fellow, somewhat entertained. "Ninety—a hundred." He shook his head and smiled. The officer at last came to three hundred tomans, (nearly one thousand dollars). "Well," said the Arab, "you need not tempt me further. You are a rich nobleman, and, I am told, have loads of silver and gold. Now," added he, "you want my mare, but you shall not have her for all you have got." He put spurs to his horse, and was soon out of the reach of temptation.

14. The horse can swim, when necessary, as well as most other animals, although he is not very fond of the water. Some years ago a vessel was driven upon the rocks, on the coast of the Cape of Good Hope, and most of the crew fell an immediate sacrifice to the waves. Those who were left were seen from the shore, clinging to the different pieces of the wreck. The sea ran so high that no boat could venture off to their assistance.

15. Meanwhile, a planter had come from his farm to be a spectator of the shipwreck. His heart was melted at the sight of the unhappy seamen, and, knowing the bold spirit of his horse and his excellence as a swimmer, he determined to make a desperate effort for their deliverance. Having blown a little Brandy into his horse's nostrils, he pushed into the midst of the breakers. At first both horse and rider disappeared, but it was not long before they floated to the surface, and swam up to the wreck; when, taking two men

with him, each of whom held on by one of his boots, the planter brought them safe to shore.

16. This was repeated no less than seven times, and he saved fourteen lives; but on his return the eighth time, being much fatigued, and meeting a tremendous wave, he lost his balance and sank in a moment. His horse swam safely to land, but its gallant rider sank, to rise no more.

Definitions.—4. Im-mĕnse′, *very large*. In-hăb′it-ed, *occupied as a home*. Căv′al-ry, *a body of military troops on horses*. 5. Im-pĕt-ū-ŏs′i-ty, *fury, violence*. 8. Dĕx′ter-oŭs-ly, *skillfully*. 9. Re-dūçed′, *brought into*. 10. O-rĭg′i-nal-ly, *at first*. 12. Pa-rād′ed, *showed off*. 8. Sўm′me-try, *a proper proportion of the several parts*. 13. To-män′, *a Persian coin valued at about three dollars*. 15. Dĕs′per-ate, *without care of safety*. De-lĭv′er-ançe, *release from danger*. 16. Găl′lant, *brave, heroic*.

Exercises.—Where are wild horses found? How are they taken? For what purpose are they taken? In what country are the finest horses raised? Why are the horses so excellent there? Are not animals always made better by kind treatment? Why would not the Arab sell his horse? Relate the anecdote of the planter and the shipwrecked seamen.

XLVIII. EMULATION.

1. Frank's father was speaking to a friend, one day, on the subject of competition at school. He said that he could answer for it that envy is not always connected with it.

2. He had been excelled by many, but did not recollect ever having felt envious of his successful rivals; "nor did my winning many a prize from my

friend Birch," said he, "ever lessen his friendship for me."

3. In support of the truth of this, a friend who was present related an anecdote which had fallen under his own notice in a school in his neighborhood.

4. At this school the sons of several wealthy farmers, and others, who were poorer, received instruction. Frank listened with great attention while the gentleman gave the following account of the two rivals:

5. It happened that the son of a rich farmer and the son of a poor widow came in competition for the head of their class. They were so nearly equal that the teacher could scarcely decide between them; some days one, and some days the other, gained the head of the class. It was determined by seeing who should be at the head of the class for the greater number of days in the week.

6. The widow's son, by the last day's trial, gained the victory, and kept his place the following week, till the school was dismissed for the holidays.

7. When they met again the widow's son did not appear, and the farmer's son, being next to him, might now have been at the head of his class. Instead of seizing the vacant place, however, he went to the widow's house to inquire what could be the cause of her son's absence.

8. Poverty was the cause; the poor woman found that she was not able, with her utmost efforts, to continue to pay for the tuition and books of her son, and so he, poor fellow! had been compelled to give up his schooling, and to return to labor for her support.

9. The farmer's son, out of the allowance of pocket money which his father gave him, bought all the necessary books and paid for the tuition of his rival. He

also permitted him to be brought back again to the head of his class, where he continued for some time, at the expense of his generous rival.

DEFINITIONS.—Em-u-lā´tion, *rivalry, contest.* 1. Cŏm-pe-tĭ´tion, *rivalry.* 2. Ex-çĕlled´, *surpassed, exceeded in good qualities.* Rī´valṣ, *those who pursue the same thing.* 3. An´ec-dōte, *a short story.* 8. Tu-ĭ´tion, *payment for teaching.*

EXERCISES.—What is the subject of this lesson? What do you mean by emulation? What is envy? What story is told about the two rivals? Is it right to envy any person?

XLIX. THE SANDPIPER.

By CELIA THAXTER.

1. Across the lonely beach we flit,
      One little sandpiper and I,
   And fast I gather, bit by bit,
      The scattered driftwood, bleached and dry.
   The wild waves reach their hands for it,
      The wild wind raves, the tide runs high,
   As up and down the beach we flit,
      One little sandpiper and I.

2. Above our heads the sullen clouds
      Scud, black and swift, across the sky;
   Like silent ghosts in misty shrouds
      Stand out the white lighthouses high.
   Almost as far as eye can reach
      I see the close-reefed vessels fly,
   As fast we flit across the beach,
      One little sandpiper and I.

3. I watch him as he skims along,
 Uttering his sweet and mournful cry;
He starts not at my fitful song,
 Nor flash of fluttering drapery.
He has no thought of any wrong,
 He scans me with a fearless eye;
Stanch friends are we, well-tried and strong,
 The little sandpiper and I.

4. Comrade, where wilt thou be to-night,
 When the loosed storm breaks furiously?
My driftwood fire will burn so bright!
 To what warm shelter canst thou fly?
I do not fear for thee, though wroth
 The tempest rushes through the sky;
For are we not God's children both,
 Thou, little sandpiper, and I?

DEFINITIONS.—1. Sănd′pī-per, *a bird of the snipe family, found along the seacoast.* Drĭft′wood, *wood tossed on shore by the waves.* Blēached, *whitened.* Tīde, *the regular rise and fall of the ocean which occurs twice in a little over twenty-four hours.* 2. Scŭd, *fly hastily.* Shrouds, *winding sheets, dresses of the dead.* Clōse′reefed, *with sails contracted as much as possible.* 3. Fĭt′ful, *irregularly variable.* Drā′per-y, *garments.* Scăns, *looks at carefully.* Stănch, *firm.* 4. Wrôth, *angry.*

L. THE RIGHT WAY.

Adapted from a story by **Frank H. Stockton.** He was born at Philadelphia, April 5, 1834, and when quite a young boy used to write stories for his own pleasure. He was once a designer and engraver on wood, and afterwards an editor; but he now devotes himself entirely to writing, not only for young but also for grown people.

1. "O Andy!" said little Jenny Murdock, "I'm so glad you came along this way. I can't get over."

2. "Can't get over?" said Andrew. "Why what's the matter?"

3. "The bridge is gone," said Jenny. "When I came across after breakfast it was there, and now it's over on the other side, and how can I get back home?"

4. "Why, so it is," said Andrew. "It was all right when I came over a little while ago, but old Donald pulls it on the other side every morning after he has driven his cows across, and I don't think he has any right to do it. I suppose he thinks the bridge was made for him and his cows."

5. "Now I must go down to the big bridge, Andy, and I want you to go with me. I'm afraid to go through all those dark woods by myself," said Jenny.

6. "But I can't go, Jenny," said Andrew, "it's nearly school time now."

7. Andrew was a Scotch boy, and a fine fellow. He was next to the head of his school, and he was as good at play as he was at his book.

8. Jenny Murdock, his most particular friend, was a little girl who lived very near Andrew's home. She had no brothers or sisters, but Andrew had always been as good as a brother to her; and, therefore, when

she stood by the water's edge that morning, just ready to burst into tears, she thought all her troubles over when she saw Andrew coming along the road.

9. He had always helped her out of her troubles before, and she saw no reason why he should not do it now. She had crossed the creek in search of wild flowers, and when she wished to return had found the bridge removed, as Andrew supposed, by old Donald McKensie, who pastured his cows on this side of the creek.

10. This stream was not very wide, nor very deep at its edges, but the center it was four or five feet deep; and in the spring the water ran very swiftly, so that wading across it, either by cattle or men, was quite a difficult undertaking. As for Jenny, she could not get across at all without a bridge, and there was none nearer than the wagon bridge, a mile and a half below.

11. "You will go with me, Andy, won't you?" said the little girl.

12. "And be late to school?" said he. "I have not been late yet, you know, Jenny."

13. "Perhaps Dominie Black will think you have been sick or had to mind the cows," said Jenny.

14. "He won't think so unless I tell him," said Andrew, "and you know I won't do that."

15. "If we were to run all the way, would you be too late?" said Jenny.

16. "If we were to run all the way to the bridge, and I were to run all the way back, I should not get to school till after copy time. I expect every minute to hear the school bell ring," said Andrew.

17. "But what can I do, then?" said poor little Jenny. "I can't wait here till school's out, and I

don't want to go up to the schoolhouse, for all the boys to laugh at me."

18. "No," said Andrew, reflecting very seriously, "I must take you home some way or other. It won't do to leave you here, and, no matter where you might stay, your mother would be very much troubled about you."

19. "Yes," said Jenny, "she would think I was drowned."

20. Time pressed, and Jenny's countenance became more and more overcast, but Andrew could think of no way in which he could take the little girl home without being late and losing his standing in the school.

21. It was impossible to get her across the stream at any place nearer than the "big bridge;" he would not take her that way, and make up a false story to account for his lateness at school, and he could not leave her alone or take her with him.

22. What was to be done? While several absurd and impracticable plans were passing through his brain, the school bell began to ring, and he must start immediately to reach the schoolhouse in time.

23. And now his anxiety and perplexity became more intense than ever; and Jenny, looking up into his troubled countenance, began to cry.

24. Andrew, who had never before failed to be at the school door before the first tap of the bell, began to despair. Was there nothing to be done?

25. Yes! a happy thought passed through his mind. How strange that he should not have thought of it before! He would ask Dominie Black to let him take Jenny home. What could be more sensible and straightforward than such a plan?

26. Of course the good old schoolmaster gave Andrew the desired permission, and every thing ended happily. But the best thing about the whole affair was the lesson that the young Scotch boy learned that day.

27. The lesson was this: when we are puzzling our brains with plans to help ourselves out of trouble, let us always stop a moment in our planning, and try to think if there is not some simple way out of the difficulty, which shall be in every respect perfectly right. If we do this, we shall probably find a way more easy and satisfactory than any which we can devise.

DEFINITIONS.—8. Par-tĭe'ū-lar, *not ordinary, worthy of particular attention, chief.* 13. Dŏm'i-nĭe, *the Scotch name for school-master.* 18. Re-flĕet'ing, *thinking earnestly.* 20 Over-eäst', *covered with gloom.* 21. Ae-eount', *to state the reasons.* 22. Im-prăe'ti-ca-ble, *not possible.* 23. Anx-ī'e-ty, *care, trouble of mind.* 27. De-vīṣe', *plan, contrive.*

EXERCISES.—Why could not Jenny cross the stream? Whom did she ask to help her? What can you tell about Andrew? Who was Jenny Murdock? What did Jenny wish Andrew to do? Why could he not go with her? Would it have been right for Andrew to have told an untruth even to help Jenny out of trouble? What did he finally do? What does this lesson teach us to do in case of trouble?

LI. THE GOLDEN RULE.

1. To act with integrity and good faith was such a habit with Susan that she had never before thought of examining the Golden Rule: "All things whatsoever ye would that men should do to you, do ye even so to them." But the longer she reflected upon it, the

stronger was her conviction that she did not always obey the precept; at length, she appealed to her mother for its meaning.

2. "It implies," said her mother, "in the first place, a total destruction of all selfishness: for a man who loves himself better than his neighbors, can never do to others as he would have others do to him. We are bound not only to do, but to feel, toward others as we would have others feel toward us. Remember, it is much easier to reprove the sin of others than to overcome temptation when it assails ourselves.

3. "A man may be perfectly honest and yet very selfish; but the command implies something more than mere honesty; it requires charity as well as integrity. The meaning of the command is fully explained in the parable of the Good Samaritan. The Levite, who passed by the wounded man without offering him assistance, may have been a man of great honesty; but he did not do unto the poor stranger as he would have wished others to do unto him."

4. Susan pondered carefully and seriously on what her mother had said. When she thought over her past conduct, a blush of shame crept to her cheeks, and a look of sorrow into her eyes, as many little acts of selfishness and unkindness came back to her memory. She resolved that for the future, both in great things and small, she would remember and follow the Golden Rule.

5. It was not long after this that an opportunity occurred of trying Susan's principles. One Saturday evening when she went, as usual, to farmer Thompson's inn, to receive the price of her mother's washing for the boarders, which amounted to five dollars, she found the farmer in the stable yard.

6. He was apparently in a terrible rage with some horse dealers with whom he had been bargaining. He held in his hand an open pocketbook, full of bills; and scarcely noticing the child as she made her request, except to swear at her, as usual, for troubling him when he was busy, he handed her a bank note.

7. Glad to escape so easily, Susan hurried out of the gate, and then, pausing to pin the money safely in the folds of her shawl, she discovered that he had given her two bills instead of one. She looked around; nobody was near to share her discovery; and her first impulse was joy at the unexpected prize.

8. "It is mine, all mine," said she to herself; "I will buy mother a new cloak with it, and she can give her old one to sister Mary, and then Mary can go to the Sunday school with me next winter. I wonder if it will not buy a pair of shoes for brother Tom, too."

9. At that moment she remembered that he must have given it to her by mistake; and therefore she had no right to it. But again the voice of the tempter whispered, "He gave it, and how do you know that he did not intend to make you a present of it? Keep it; he will never know it, even if it should be a mistake; for he had too many such bills in that great pocketbook to miss one."

10. While this conflict was going on in her mind between good and evil, she was hurrying homeward as fast as possible. Yet, before she came in sight of her home, she had repeatedly balanced the comforts which the money would buy against the sin of wronging her neighbor.

11. As she crossed the little bridge over the narrow creek before her mother's door, her eye fell upon a

rustic seat which they had occupied during the conversation I have before narrated. Instantly the words of
Scripture, "Whatsoever ye would that men should
do to you, do ye even so to them," sounded in her ears
like a trumpet.

12. Turning suddenly round, as if flying from some
unseen peril, the child hastened along the road with
breathless speed until she found herself once more at
farmer Thompson's gate. "What do you want now?"
asked the gruff old fellow, as he saw her again at his
side.

13. "Sir, you paid me two bills, instead of one,"
said she, trembling in every limb. "Two bills? did
I? let me see; well, so I did; but did you just find it out?
Why did you not bring it back sooner?" Susan blushed
and hung her head.

14. "You wanted to keep it, I suppose," said he.
"Well, I am glad your mother was more honest than
you, or I should have been five dollars poorer and
none the wiser." "My mother knows nothing about
it, sir," said Susan; "I brought it back before I went
home."

15. The old man looked at the child, and, as he saw
the tears rolling down her checks, he seemed touched
by her distress. Putting his band in his pocket, he drew
out a shilling and offered it to her.

16. "No, sir, I thank you," sobbed she; "I do not
want to be paid for doing right; I only wish you would
not think me dishonest, for, indeed, it was a sore temptation. Oh! sir, if you had ever seen those you love best
wanting the common comforts of life, you would
know how hard it is for us always to do unto others as
we would have others do unto us,"

17. The heart of the selfish man was touched.

"There be things which are little upon the earth, but they are exceeding wise," murmured he, as he bade the little girl good night, and entered his house a sadder, and, it is to be hoped, a better man. Susan returned to her humble home with a lightened heart, and through the course of a long and useful life she never forgot her first temptation.

DEFINITIONS.—1. In-tĕg´ri-ty, *honesty, uprightness.* Con-vĭc´tion, *strong belief.* Ap-pēaled´, *referred to.* 2. Temp-tā´tion, *that which has a tendency to induce one to do wrong.* As-sails´, *attacks.* 10. Cŏn´flict, *struggle.* Băl´ançed, *weighed, compared.* 12. Grŭff, *rough.* 17. Mŭr´mured, *spoke in a low voice.* Līght´ened, *made cheerful or lighter.*

Exercises.—What is the Golden Rule? What does it imply? Can a man be perfectly honest and still not follow the Golden Rule? What parable is a perfect illustration of its meaning? How was Susan tempted? What did she first think of doing? What changed her intention? Relate what happened when she returned the money. What effect did her action have?

LII. THE SNOW MAN.

BY MARIAN DOUGLAS.

1. Look! how the clouds are flying south!
 The winds pipe loud and shrill!
And high above the white drifts stands
 The snow man on the hill.

2. Blow, wild wind from the icy north!
 Here's one who will not fear
To feel thy coldest touch, or shrink
 Thy loudest blast to hear.

3. Proud triumph of the schoolboy's skill!
    Far rather would I be
A winter giant, ruling o'er
    A frosty realm, like thee,

4. And stand amid the drifted snow,
    Like thee, a thing apart,
Than be a man who walks with men,
    But has a frozen heart!

DEFINITIONS.—1. Pīpe, *whistle*. 2. Shrĭnk, *to draw back on account of fear.* 3. Trī´umph, *success causing exultation.* Rĕalm, *the territory over which authority is used, dominion.*

EXERCISES.—With what is the snow man compared in this poem? What is meant by a man with "a frozen heart"? Do you think such a man would follow the Golden Rule?

LIII. ROBINSON CRUSOE'S HOUSE.

Daniel DeFoe, the author of "Robinson Crusoe" (from which these selections are adapted), was born in London, England, in 1661, and died in 1731. He wrote a number of books; but his "Robinson Crusoe" is the only one that attained great notoriety.

1. I have already described my habitation, which was a tent under the side of a rock, surrounded with a strong pale of posts and cables, but I might now rather call it a wall, for I raised a kind of wall up against it of turf, about two feet thick on the outside; and, after some time (I think it was a year and a half) I raised rafters from it, leaning to the rock, and thatched or covered it with boughs of trees and such things as I could get to keep out the rain, which I found at some times of the year very violent.

2. I have already observed how I brought all my goods into this pale, and into the cave which I had made behind me; but I must observe, too, that at first this was a confused heap of goods, which, as they lay in no order, took up all my place, so that I had no room to turn myself. So I set to work to enlarge my cave and work farther into the earth; for it was a loose, sandy rock, which yielded easily to the labor I bestowed upon it.

3. And so when I found that I was pretty safe as to beasts of prey, I worked sideways into the rock; and then, turning to the right again, worked quite out, and made me a door to come out on the outside of my pale or fortification. This gave me not only egress and regress, as it was a back way to my tent and to my storehouse, but gave me room to stow my goods.

4. And now I began to apply myself to make such necessary things as I found I most wanted, particularly a chair and a table; for without these I was not able to enjoy the few comforts I had in the world. I could not write or eat, or do several things with so much pleasure without a table.

5. So I went to work. I had never handled a tool in my life; and yet in time by labor, application, and contrivance, I found that I wanted nothing but I could have made it, especially if I had had tools; however, I made abundance of things, even without tools, and some with no more tools than an adz and a hatchet, which perhaps were never made that way before, and that with infinite labor.

6. For example, if I wanted a board, I had no other way but to cut down a tree, set it before me, and hew it flat on either side with my ax till I had

brought it to be as thin as a plank, and then dub it smooth with my adz.

7. It is true, by this method I could make but one board out of a whole tree; but this I had no remedy for but patience, any more than I had for the prodigious deal of time and labor which it took me to make a plank or board; but my time or labor was little worth, and so it was as well employed one way as another.

8. However, I made me a table and a chair, as I observed above; and this I did out of the short pieces of boards which I brought on my raft from the ship; but when I had wrought out some boards, as above, I made large shelves, of the breadth of a foot and a half, one over another, all along one side of my cave, to lay all my tools, nails, and ironwork on, and, in a word, to separate everything at large in their places, that I might come easily at them.

9. I knocked pieces into the wall of the rock to hang my guns and all things that would hang up. So that, had my cave been seen, it would have looked like a general magazine of all necessary things; and I had everything so ready at my hand that it was a great pleasure to me to see all my goods in such order, and especially to find my stock of all necessaries so great.

DEFINITIONS.—1. Hăb-i-tā′tion, *a dwelling place*. Pāle, *a fence*. Cā′bleṣ, *large ropes*. Tûrf, *sod*. 3. Fôr-ti-fi-€ā′tion, *a place built for defense against attack*. E′ḡress, *going out*. Rē′ḡress, *coming back, return*. Stōw, *to arrange compactly*. 4. Ap-plȳ′, *to employ diligently*. 6. Dŭb, *to cut down or bring to an even surface*. 7. Pro-dĭḡ′ioŭs, *very great*. Dēal, *part, amount*. 9. Măḡ-a-zïne′, *a storehouse*,

Exercises.—How did Robinson Crusoe make a house? Of what did he make a chair and table? How did he obtain boards? What does this lesson teach us in regard to perseverance?

LIV. ROBINSON CRUSOE'S DRESS.

1. But had any man in England met such a man as I was, it must either have frightened him or raised a great deal of laughter; and, as I frequently stood still to look at myself, I could not but smile at the notion of my traveling through Yorkshire in such a dress.

2. I had a great, high, shapeless cap, made of a goat's skin, with a flap hanging down behind, as well to keep the sun from me as to shoot the rain off from running into my neck; nothing being so hurtful in these climates as the rain upon the flesh under the clothes.

3. I had a short jacket of goatskin, the skirts coming down to about the middle of the thighs, and a pair of open-kneed breeches of the same; the breeches were made of the skin of an old goat, and the hair hung down such a length on either side that it reached to the middle of my legs like pantaloons.

4. Stockings and shoes I had none; but I made a pair of something, I scarce know what to call them, like buskins, to flap over my legs, and lace on either side like spatterdashes; but they were of a most barbarous shape, as indeed were all the rest of my clothes.

5. I had on a broad belt of goatskin dried, which I drew together with two thongs of the same, instead of buckles; and, in a kind of frog on each side of this, instead of a sword and dagger, hung a little saw and hatchet; one on one side, and one on the other. I had another belt not so broad, and fastened in the same manner, which hung over my shoulder; and at the end of it, under my left arm, hung two pouches, both made of goatskin, too; in one of which hung my powder, in the other my shot.

6. At my back I carried my basket, on my shoulder my gun, and over my head a great, clumsy, ugly, goatskin umbrella, but which, after all, was the most necessary thing I had about me, next to my gun.

7. As for my face, the color of it was really not so dark as one might expect from a man not at all care-

ful of it, and living within nine or ten degrees of the equator. My beard I had once suffered to grow till it was about a quarter of a yard long; but, as I had both scissors and razors sufficient, I had cut it pretty short, except what grew on my upper lip, which I had trimmed into a large pair of Mahometan whiskers, such as I had seen worn by some Turks.

8. Of these mustaches or whiskers, I will not say that they were long enough to hang my hat upon them, but they were of a length and shape monstrous enough, and such as in England would have passed for frightful. But all this is by the bye; for, as to my figure, I had so few to observe me that it was of no manner of consequence; so I say no more on that part.

DEFINITIONS.—4. Bŭs′kins, *coverings for the feet coming some distance up the leg, and fit for a defense against thorns, etc.* Spăt′-ter-dăsh-es, *coverings for the legs to keep them clean from water and mud.* Bär′ba-roŭs, *uncouth, clumsy.* 5. Thŏngs, *strips of leather.* Frŏğ, *a loop similar to that sometimes used in fastening a cloak or coat.* Pouch′es, *bags.* 8. Mŏn′stroŭs, *very large, enormous.*

NOTES.—The novel, "Robinson Crusoe," was first published in 1719. It was founded on the adventures of Alexander Selkirk, a Scotch buccaneer, who was cast on the island of Juan Fernandez, west of South America, in 1704, and remained there for more than four years, before he was rescued.

1. *Yorkshire.* This was the district of England where, according to the story, Robinson Crusoe was born and passed his early life.

3. *Open-kneed breeches.* At this period knee breeches were worn almost altogether in England. Those referred to here appear to have been loose about the knee, and not close, as usual.

5. *Instead of sword and dagger.* It was then the fashion in England for gentlemen to wear such weapons.

8. *Such as in England would have passed for frightful.* It was not the custom in England, in DeFoe's time, to wear a full beard.

LV. SOMEBODY'S DARLING.

1. Into a ward of the whitewashed halls,
    Where the dead and dying lay,
  Wounded by bayonets, shells, and balls,
    Somebody's darling was borne one day;

2. Somebody's darling, so young and brave,
    Wearing yet on his pale, sweet face,
  Soon to be hid by the dust of the grave,
    The lingering light of his boyhood's grace.

3. Matted and damp are the curls of gold,
    Kissing the snow of that fair young brow;
  Pale are the lips of delicate mold
    Somebody's darling is dying now.

4. Back from his beautiful, blue-veined brow,
    Brush all the wandering waves of gold;
  Cross his hands on his bosom now;
    Somebody's darling is still and cold.

5. Kiss him once for somebody's sake,
    Murmur a prayer soft and low;
  One bright curl from its fair mates take;
    They were somebody's pride, you know;

6. Somebody's hand has rested there;
    Was it a mother's, soft and white?
  And have the lips of a sister fair
    Been baptized in the waves of light?

7. God knows best! he was somebody's love:
   Somebody's heart enshrined him there;
Somebody wafted his name above,
   Night and morn, on the wings of prayer.

8. Somebody wept when he marched away,
   Looking so handsome, brave, and grand;
Somebody's kiss on his forehead lay;
   Somebody clung to his parting hand.

9. Somebody's watching and waiting for him,
   Yearning to hold him again to her heart;
And there he lies, with his blue eyes dim,
   And the smiling, childlike lips apart.

10. Tenderly bury the fair young dead,
    Pausing too drop on his grave a tear;
Carve on the wooden slab at his head,
    "Somebody's darling slumbers here."

DEFINITIONS.—1. Bāy′o-net, *a short, pointed iron weapon, fitted to the muzzle of a gun.* Där′ling, *one dearly loved.* 2. Lĭn′ğer-ing, *protracted.* 3. Măt′ted, *twisted together.* Dĕl′i-cate, *soft and fair.* Mōld, *shape.* 4. Wạn′der-ing, *straying.* 7. En-shrīned′, *cherished.* Wăft′ed, *caused to float.* 9. Yĕarn′ing, *being eager, longing.* 10. Tĕn′der-ly, *gently, kindly.*

LVI. KNOWLEDGE IS POWER.

1. "What an excellent thing is knowledge," said a sharp-looking, hustling little man, to one who was much older than himself. "Knowledge is an excellent thing," repeated he. "My boys know more at six and seven years old than I did at twelve. They can read

all sorts of books, and talk on all sorts of subjects. The world is a great deal wiser than it used to he. Everybody knows something of everything now. Do you not think, sir, that knowledge is all excellent thing?"

2. "Why, sir," replied the old man, looking grave, "that depends entirely upon the use to which it is applied. It may be a blessing or a curse. Knowledge is only an increase of power, and power may be a bad, as well as a good thing." "That is what I can not understand," said the bustling little man. "How can power he a bad thing?"

3. "I will tell you," meekly replied the old man; and thus he went on: "When the power of a horse is under restraint, the animal is useful in bearing burdens, drawing loads, and carrying his master; but when that power is unrestrained, the horse breaks his bridle, dashes to pieces the carriage that he draws, or throws his rider." "I see!" said the little man.

4. "When the water of a large pond is properly conducted by trenches, it renders the fields around fertile; but when it bursts through its banks, it sweeps everything before it and destroys the produce of the fields." "I see!" said the little man, "I see!"

5. "When the ship is steered aright, the sail that she hoists enables her sooner to get into port; but if steered wrong, the more sail she carries the further will she go out of her course." "I see!" said the little man, "I see clearly!"

6. "Well, then," continued the old man, "if you see these things so clearly, I hope you can see, too, that knowledge, to be a good thing, must be rightly applied. God's grace in the heart will render the

the knowledge of the head a blessing; but without this, it may prove to us no better than a curse." "I see! I see!" said the little man, "I see!"

DEFINITIONS.—1. Bŭs'tling, *very active, stirring.* Sŭb'jeet, *the thing treated of.* 3. Meek'ly, *mildly, quietly, gently.* Re-strāint', *anything which hinders.* Bûr'dens, *loads.* 4. Con-dŭet'ed, *led, guided.* Trĕnch'eṣ, *ditches.* Fẽr'tĭle, *producing much fruit, rich.* Prŏd'ūçe, *that which is yielded or produced.* 5. Steered', *guided, directed.* Hoists, *raises.* 6. Ap-plīed', *directed, made use of.*

Exercises—What is the subject of this lesson? Is knowledge always a power? Is it always blessing? Relate the several examples of power wrongly used. If we use the powers that God has given us for bad purposes, what will our knowledge prove to be?

LVII. GOOD WILL.

BY J. T. TROWBRIDGE.—(ADAPTED)

1. I suppose you all, my boys, are looking for some sort of success in life; it is right that you should; but what are your notions of success? To get rich as soon as possible, without regard to the means by which your wealth is acquired?

2. There is no true success in that: when you have gained millions, you may yet be poorer than when you had nothing; and it is that same reckless ambition which has brought many a bright and capable boy, not to great estate at last, but to miserable failure and disgrace; not to a palace, but to a prison.

3. Wealth rightly got and rightly used, rational enjoyment, power, fame,—these are all worthy objects of ambition; but they are not the highest objects, and

you may acquire them all without achieving true success. But if, whatever you seek, you put good-will into all your actions, you are sure of the best success at last; for whatever else you gain or miss, you are building up a noble and beautiful character, which is not only the best of possessions in this world, but also is about all you can expect to take with you into the next.

4. I say, good will in all your actions. You are not simply to be kind and helpful to others; but, whatever you do, give honest, earnest purpose to it. Thomas is put by his parents to learn a business. But Thomas does not like to apply himself very closely. "What's the use?" he says. "I'm not paid much, and I'm not going to work much. I'll get along just as easily as I can, and have as good times as I can."

5. So he shirks his tasks; and instead of thinking about his employer's interests, or his own self improvement, gives his mind to trifles,—often to evil things, which in their ruinous effects upon his life are not trifles. As soon as he is free from his daily duties, he is off with his companions, having what they call a good time; his heart is with them even while his hands are employed in the shop or store.

6. He does nothing thoroughly well,—not at all for want of talent, but solely for lack of good will. He is not preparing himself to be one of those efficient clerks or workmen who are always in demand, and who receive the highest wages.

7. There is a class of people who are the pest of every community, workmen who do not know their trade, men of business ignorant of the first principles of business. They can never be relied upon to do

well anything they undertake. They are always making blunders which other people have to suffer for, and which react upon themselves. They are always getting out of employment, and failing in business.

8. To make up for what they lack in knowledge and thoroughness, they often resort to trick and fraud, and become not merely contemptible but criminal. Thomas is preparing himself to be one of this class. You can not, boys, expect to raise a good crop from evil seed.

9. By Thomas's side works another boy, whom we will call James,—a lad of only ordinary capacity, very likely. If Thomas and all the other boys did their best, there would be but small chance for James ever to become eminent. But he has something better than talent: he brings good will to his work. Whatever he learns, he learns so well that it becomes a part of himself.

10. His employers find that they can depend upon Jim. Customers soon learn to like and trust him. By diligence, self-culture, good habits, cheerful and kindly conduct, he is laying the foundation of a generous manhood and a genuine success.

11. In short, boys, by slighting your tasks you hurt yourself more than you wrong your employer. By honest service you benefit yourself more than you help him. If you were aiming at mere worldly advancement only, I should still say that good will was the very best investment you could make in business.

12. By cheating a customer, you gain only a temporary and unreal advantage. By serving him with right good will,—doing by him as you would be done by,—you not only secure his confidence but also his good will in return. But this is a sordid considera-

ation compared with the inward satisfaction, the glow and expansion of soul which attend a good action done for itself alone. If I were to sum up all I have to say to you in one last word of love and counsel, that one word should be—Good will.

DEFINITIONS.—3. Chăr'ăe-ter, *the sum of qualities which distinguish one person from another.* 4. Pŭr'pŏse, *intention, aim.* 7. Prĭn'çi-ples, *fixed rules.* 9. Ca-păç'i-ty, *ability, the power of receiving ideas.* 12. Sôr'did, *base, meanly avaricious.*

Exercises.—What is meant by the phrase "to apply himself," in the fourth paragraph? What is meant by "a generous manhood," tenth paragraph? By "expansion of soul," twelfth paragraph? Tell what is meant by "good will," as taught by this lesson. How did Tom and James differ in character?

LVIII. A CHINESE STORY. (156)

By **Christopher Pearse Cranch**, who was born at Alexandria, Va. (then D. C.), in 1813. He has written some well-known children's stories, besides numerous poems; but his greatest literary work is "The Æneid of Vergil, translated into English blank verse." He died in Cambridge Mass., 1892.

1. Two young, near-sighted fellows, Chang and Ching,
   Over their chopsticks idly chattering,
   Fell to disputing which could see the best;
   At last, they agreed to put it to the test.
   Said Chang, "A marble tablet, so I hear,
   Is placed upon the Bo-hee temple near,
   With an inscription on it. Let us go
   And read it (since you boast your optics so),
   Standing together at a certain place
   In front, where we the letters just may trace;
   Then he who quickest reads the inscription there,

The palm for keenest eyes henceforth shall bear."
"Agreed," said Ching, "but let us try it soon:
Suppose we say to-morrow afternoon."

2. "Nay, not so soon," said Chang; "I'm bound to go
    To-morrow a day's ride from Hoang-Ho,
    And sha'n't be ready till the following day:
    At ten A. M., on Thursday, let us say."

3. So 'twas arranged; but Ching was wide-awake:
    Time by the forelock he resolved to take;
    And to the temple went at once, and read,
    Upon the tablet, "To the illustrious dead,
    The chief of mandarins, the great Goh-Bang."
    Scarce had he gone when stealthily came Chang,
    Who read the same; but peering closer, he
    Spied in a corner what Ching failed to see—
    The words, "This tablet is erected here
    By those to whom the great Goh-Bang was dear."

4. So on the appointed day—both innocent
    As babes, of course—these honest fellows went,
    And took their distant station; and Ching said,
    "I can read plainly, 'To the illustrious dead,
    The chief of mandarins, the great Goh-Bang.'"
    "And is that all that you can spell?" said Chang;
    "I see what you have read, but furthermore,
    In smaller letters, toward the temple door,
    Quite plain, 'This tablet is erected here
    By those to whom the great Goh-Bang was dear.'"

5. "My sharp-eyed friend, there are no such words!"
        said Ching.
    "They're there," said Chang, "if I see anything,

As clear as daylight." "Patent eyes, indeed,
You have!" cried Ching; "do you think I can not
   read?"
Not at this distance as I can," Chang said,
"If what you say you saw is all you read."

6. In fine, they quarreled, and their wrath increased,
   Till Chang said, "Let us leave it to the priest;
   Lo! here he comes to meet us," "It is well,"
   Said honest Ching; "no falsehood he will tell."

7. The good man heard their artless story through,
And said, "I think, dear sirs, there must be few
Blest with such wondrous eyes as those you wear:
There's no such tablet or inscription there!
There was one, it is true; 't was moved away
And placed within the temple yesterday."

DEFINITIONS.—1. Nēar-sīght′ed, *seeing at a short distance only.* Chŏp′stĭcks, *small sticks of wood, ivory, etc., used in pairs by Chinese to carry food to the mouth.* Tăb′let, *a small, flat piece of anything on which to write or engrave.* In-scrĭp′tion, *something written or engraved on a solid substance.* Op′tics, *eyes.* Palm, *the reward of victory, prize.* 2. A. M., *an abbreviation for the Latin ante meridian, meaning before noon.* 3. Măn-da-rïn′, *a Chinese public officer.* 5. Păt′ent, *secured from general use, peculiar to one person.*

LXX. THE WAY TO BE HAPPY.

1. Every child must observe how much more happy and beloved some children are than others. There are some children you always love to be with. They are happy themselves, and they make you happy.

2. There are others whom you always avoid. They seem to have no friends. No person can be happy without friends. The heart is formed for love, and can not be happy without it.

3.
"'Tis not in titles nor in rank,
'Tis not in wealth like London bank,
To make us truly blest.
If happiness have not her seat
And center in the breast,
We may be wise, or rich, or great,
But never can be blest."

4. But you can not receive affection unless you will also give it. You can not find others to love you unless you will also love them. Love is only to be obtained by giving love in return. Hence the importance of cultivating a good disposition. You can not be happy without it.

5. I have sometimes heard a girl say, "I know that I am very unpopular at school." Now, this plainly shows that she is not amiable.

6. If your companions do not love you, it is your own fault. They can not help loving you if you will be kind and friendly. If you are not loved, it is a good proof that you do not deserve to be loved. It is true that a sense of duty may, at times, render it necessary for you to do that which will displease your companions.

7. But if it is seen that you have a noble spirit, that you are above selfishness, that you are willing to make sacrifices to promote the happiness of others, you will never be in want of friends.

8. You must not regard it as your misfortune that others do not love you, but your fault. It is not beauty, it is not wealth, that will give you friends. Your heart must glow with kindness, if you would attract to yourself the esteem and affection of those around you.

9. You are little aware how much the happiness of your whole life depends upon the cultivation of a good disposition. If you will adopt the resolution that you will confer favors whenever you can, you will certainly be surrounded by ardent friends. Begin upon this principle in childhood, and act upon it through life, and you will make yourself happy, and promote the happiness of all within your influence.

10. You go to school on a cold winter morning. A bright fire is blazing in the stove, surrounded with boys struggling to get near it to warm themselves. After you are slightly warmed, a schoolmate comes in suffering with cold. "Here, James," you pleasantly call out to him, "I am almost warm; you may have my place."

11. As you slip aside to allow him to take your place at the fire, will he not feel that you are kind? The worst boy in the world can not help admiring such generosity; and, even though he be so ungrateful as not to return the favor, you may depend upon it that he will be your friend as far as he is capable of friendship. If you will always act upon this principle, you will never want for friends.

12. Suppose, some day, you are out with your companions playing ball. After you have been playing for some time, another boy comes along. He can not be chosen upon either side, for there is no one to match him. "Henry," you say, "you may take my place a little while, and I will rest."

13. You throw yourself down upon the grass, while Henry, fresh and vigorous, takes your bat and engages in the game. He knows that you give up to oblige him, and how can he help liking you for it? The fact is, that neither man nor child can cultivate such a spirit of generosity and kindness without attracting affection and esteem.

14. Look and see which of your companions have the most friends, and you will find that they are those who have this noble spirit; who are willing to deny themselves, that they may make others happy. There is but one way to make friends; and that is, by being friendly to others.

15. Perhaps some child who reads this feels conscious of being disliked, and yet desires to have the affection of his companions. You ask me what you shall do. I will tell you. I will give you an infallible rule: Do all in your power to make others happy. Be willing to make sacrifices, that you may promote the happiness of others.

16. This is the way to make friends, and the only way. When you are playing with your brothers and sisters at home, be always ready to give them more than their share of privileges. Manifest an obliging disposition, and they can not but regard you with affection. In all your intercourse with others, at home or abroad, let these feelings influence you, and you will receive a rich reward.

DEFINITIONS.—4. Cŭl′ti-vāt-ing, *cherishing, encouraging.* 5. Un-pŏp′ū-lar, *not pleasing others.* 6. Com-păn′ionş, *those who keep company with anyone.* 7. Săċ′ri-fīc-eş, *things given up to oblige others.* Pro-mōte′, *advance, forward.* 10. Sŭf′fer-ing, *undergoing pain.* 11. Gĕn-er-ŏs′i-ty, *kindness, nobleness of soul.* 15. In-făl′li-ble, *certain, that can not fail.* 16. Măn′i-fest, *to show plainly.* In′ter-ċōurse, *communication, mutual dealings.*

Exercises.—What is this lesson about? Can we be happy without friends? How can we win the love of those about us? Whose fault is it if we are not loved? What rule will surely gain us love and friendship if we always follow it?

LX. THE GIRAFFE, OR CAMELOPARD.

1. The giraffe is a native of Africa. It is of singular shape and size, and bears some resemblance both to the camel and the deer. The mouth is small; the eyes are full and brilliant; the tongue is rough, very

long, and ending in a point. The neck is long and slender, and, from the shoulder to the top of the head, it measures between seven and eight feet; from the ground to the top of the shoulder, it is commonly ten or eleven feet; so that the height of a full-grown giraffe is seventeen or eighteen feet.

2. The hair is of a deep brown color in the male, and of a light or yellowish brown in the female. The skin is beautifully diversified with white spots. They have short, blunt horns, and hoofs like those of the ox. In their wild state, they feed on the leaves of a gum-bearing tree peculiar to warm climates.

3. The giraffe, like the horse and other hoofed animals, defends itself by kicking; and its hinder limbs are so light, and its blows so rapid, that the eye can not follow them. They are sufficient for its defense against the lion. It never employs its horns in resisting the attack of an enemy. Its disposition is gentle, and it flees to its native forest upon the least alarm.

4. Le Vaillant (the celebrated French traveler and naturalist) was the first who gave us any exact account of the form and habits of the giraffe. While he was traveling in South Africa, he happened one day to discover a hut covered with the skin of one of those animals; and learned to his surprise that he was now in a part of the country where the creature was found. He could not rest contented until he had seen the animal alive, and had secured a specimen.

5. Having on several days obtained sight of some of them, he, with his attendants, on horseback and accompanied with dogs, gave chase; but they baffled all pursuit. After a chase of a whole day, which effected nothing but the fatigue of the party, he began to despair of success.

6. "The next day," says he, "by sunrise, I was in pursuit of game, in the hope of obtaining some provisions for my men. After several hours' fatigue, we saw, at the turn of a hill, seven giraffes, which my pack of dogs instantly pursued. Six of them went off together; but the seventh, cut off by my dogs, took another way.

7. "I followed the single one at full speed, but, in spite of the efforts of my horse, she got so much ahead of me, that, in turning a little hill, I lost sight of her altogether, and I gave up the pursuit. My dogs, however, were not so easily exhausted. They were soon so close upon her that she was obliged to stop and defend herself. From the noise they made, I conjectured that they had got the animal into a corner, and I again pushed forward.

8. "I had scarcely got round the hill, when I perceived her surrounded by the dogs, and endeavoring to drive them away by heavy kicks. In a moment I was on my feet, and a shot from my carbine brought her to the earth. I was delighted with my victory, which enabled me to add to the riches of natural history. I was now able, also, to destroy the romance which attached to this animal, and to establish the truth of its existence."

DEFINITIONS.—1. Brĭl′liant, *sparkling, shining.* 2. Dĭ-vēr′si-fīed, *made various.* Pe-çūl′iar, *especially belonging to.* 4. Năt′ū-ral-ĭst, *one who is acquainted with objects of nature.* Spĕç′i-men, *a sample.* 5. Băf′fled, *defeated, escaped from.* Fa-tīgue′, *weariness.* 7. Con-jĕct′ūred, *guessed.* 8. Cär′bine, *a short gun.* Ro-mănçe′, *a story without truth.*

EXERCISES.—Of what country is the giraffe a native? To what height does it attain when full grown? On what does it live? How does it defend itself? Relate the story of Le Vaillant's giraffe hunt.

LXI. THE LOST CHILD.

1. A few years since, a child was lost in the woods. He was out with his brothers and sisters gathering berries, and was accidentally separated from them, and lost. The children, after looking in vain for some time in search of the little wanderer, returned, just in the dusk of the evening, to inform their parents that their brother was lost and could not be found.

2. The woods, at that time, were full of bears. The darkness of a cloudy night was rapidly coming on, and the alarmed father, gathering a few of his neighbors, hastened in search of the lost child. The mother remained at home, almost distracted with suspense.

3. As the clouds gathered, and the darkness increased, the father and the neighbors, with highly excited fears, traversed the woods in all directions, and raised loud shouts to attract the attention of the child. But their search was in vain. They could find no trace of the wanderer; and, as they stood under the boughs of the lofty trees, and listened, that if possible they might hear his feeble voice, no sound was borne to their ears but the melancholy moaning of the wind as it swept through the thick branches of the forest.

4. The gathering clouds threatened an approaching storm, and the deep darkness of the night had already enveloped them. It is difficult to conceive what were the feelings of that father. And who could imagine how deep the distress which filled the bosom of that mother, as she heard the wind, and beheld the darkness in which her child was wandering!

5. The search was continued in vain till nine o'clock in the evening. Then, one of the party was sent back

to the village, to collect the inhabitants for a more extensive search. The bell rung the alarm, and the cry of fire resounded through the streets. It was ascertained, however, that it was not fire which caused the alarm, but that the bell tolled the more solemn tidings of a lost child.

6. Every heart sympathized in the sorrows of the distracted parents. Soon, multitudes of the people were seen ascending the hill, upon the declivity of which the village stood, to aid in the search. Ere long, the rain began to fall, but no tidings came back to the village of the lost child. Hardly an eye was that night closed in sleep, and there was not a mother who did not feel for the parents.

7. The night passed away, and the morning dawned, and yet no tidings came. At last, those engaged in the search met together and held a consultation. They made arrangements for a more minute search, and agreed that, in case the child was found, a gun should be fired, to give a signal to the rest of the party.

8. As the sun arose, the clouds were scattered, and the whole landscape glittered in the rays of the bright morning. But that village was deserted and still. The stores were closed, and business was hushed. Mothers were walking the streets, with sympathizing countenances and anxious hearts. There was but one thought in every mind: "What has become of the lost child?"

9. All the affections and interest of the neighborhood were flowing in one deep and broad channel toward the little wanderer. About nine in the morning, the signal gun was fired, which announced that the child was found; and, for a moment, how dreadful

was the suspense! Was it found a mangled corpse? or was it alive and well?

10. Soon, a joyful shout proclaimed the safety of the child. The shout was borne from tongue to tongue, till the whole forest rang again with the joyful sound. A messenger rapidly bore the tidings to the distracted mother. A procession was immediately formed by those engaged in the search. The child was placed upon a platform, hastily formed from the boughs of trees, and borne in triumph at the head of the procession. When they arrived at the brow of the hill, they rested for a moment, and proclaimed their success with three loud and animated cheers.

11. The procession then moved on till they arrived in front of the dwelling where the parents of the child resided. The mother, who stood at the door, with streaming eyes and throbbing heart, could no longer restrain herself or her feelings.

12. She rushed into the street, clasped her child to her bosom, and wept aloud. Every eye was filled with tears, and, for a moment, all were silent. But suddenly some one gave a signal for a shout. One loud, and long, and happy note of joy rose from the assembled multitude, and they went to their business and their homes.

13. There was more joy over the one child that was found than over the ninety and nine that went not astray. Likewise, there is joy in the presence of the angels of God over one sinner that repenteth. But still, this is a feeble representation of the love of our Father in heaven for us, and of the joy with which the angels welcome the returning wanderer.

14. The mother can not feel for her child that is lost as God feels for the unhappy wanderer in the

paths of sin. If a mother can feel so much, what must be the feelings of our Father in heaven for those who have strayed from his love? If man can feel so deep a sympathy, what must be the emotions which glow in the bosom of angels?

DEFINITIONS.—1. Sĕp′a-rāt-ed, *parted.* 2. Dis-trăct′ed, *made crazy.* Sus-pĕnse′, *doubt, uncertainty.* 3. Trăv′ersed, *passed over and examined.* 5. As-çer-tāined′, *made certain.* 6. Sўm′pa-thīzed, *felt for.* De-eliv′i-ty, *descent of land.* 7. Cŏn-sul-tā′tion, *a meeting of persons to advise together.* 8. Lănd′seāpe, *a portion of territory which the eye can see in a single view.* 10. Pro-elāimed′, *made known publicly.* 11. Pro-çĕs′sion, *a train of persons walking or riding.* 13. Rĕp-re-şen-tā′tion, *the act of describing or showing.*

LXII. WHICH?

By Mrs. E. L. Beers.

1. Which shall it be? Which shall it be?
   I looked at John—John looked at me;
   Dear, patient John, who loves me yet
   As well as though my locks were jet.
   And when I found that I must speak,
   My voice seemed strangely low and weak:
   "Tell me again what Robert said!"
   And then I, listening, bent my head.
   "This is his letter:"

2. 　　　　　　　　　"'I will give
   A house and land while you shall live,
   If, in return, from out your seven,
   One child to me for aye is given.'"
   I looked at John's old garments worn,
   I thought of all that John had borne

Of poverty, and work, and care,
Which I, though willing, could not share;
I thought of seven mouths to feed,
Of seven little children's need,
And then of this.

3.   "Come, John," said I,
"We'll choose among them as they lie
Asleep;" so, walking hand in hand,
Dear John and I surveyed our band.
First to the cradle light we stepped,
Where Lilian the baby slept,
A glory 'gainst the pillow white.

Softly the father stooped to lay
His rough hand down in loving way,
When dream or whisper made her stir,
And huskily he said: "Not her!"

4. We stooped beside the trundle-bed,
   And one long ray of lamplight shed
   Athwart the boyish faces there,
   In sleep so pitiful and fair;
   I saw on Jamie's rough, red cheek,
   A tear undried. Ere John could speak,
   "He's but a baby, too," said I,
   And kissed him as we hurried by.

5. Pale, patient Robbie's angel face
   Still in his sleep bore suffering's trace:
   "No, for a thousand crowns, not him,"
   He whispered, while our eyes were dim.

6. Poor Dick! bad Dick! our wayward son,
  Turbulent, reckless, idle one—
  Could he be spared? "Nay, He who gave,
  Bade us befriend him to the grave;
  Only a mother's heart can be
  Patient enough for such as he;
  And so," said John, "I would not dare
  To send him from her bedside prayer."

7. Then stole we softly up above
  And knelt by Mary, child of love.
  "Perhaps for her 't would better be,"
  I said to John. Quite silently
  He lifted up a curl that lay
  Across her cheek in willful way,
  And shook his head. "Nay, love, not thee,"
  The while my heart beat audibly.

8. Only one more, our eldest lad,
  Trusty and truthful, good and glad
  So like his father. "No, John, no—
  I can not, will not let him go."

9. And so we wrote in courteous way,
  We could not drive one child away.
  And afterward, toil lighter seemed,
  Thinking of that of which we dreamed;
  Happy, in truth, that not one face
  We missed from its accustomed place;
  Thankful to work for all the seven,
  Trusting the rest to One in heaven!

DEFINITIONS.—2. Aye, *always.* 3. Sur-veyed', *took a view of.*
5. Crown, *an English silver coin worth about $1.20.* 6. Wāy-ward,
willful. Tûr'bu-lent, *disposed to disorder.* 9. Coûr'te-oŭs, *polite.*
Ac-cŭs'tomed, *usual.*

LXIII. THE PET FAWN.

1. A pretty little fawn had been brought in from the woods, when very young, and nursed and petted by a lady in the village until it had become as tame as possible. It was graceful, as those little creatures always are, and so gentle and playful that it became a great favorite, following the different members of the family about, being caressed by the neighbors, and welcome everywhere.

2. One morning, after playing about as usual until weary, it lay down in the sunshine, at the feet of one of its friends, upon the steps of a store. There came along a countryman, who for several years had been a hunter by pursuit, and who still kept several hounds, one of which was now with him.

3. The dog, as it approached the spot where the fawn lay, suddenly stopped. The little animal saw him, and started to its feet. It had lived more than half its life among the dogs of the village, and had apparently lost all fear of them; but it seemed now to know that an enemy was near. In an instant, its whole nature seemed changed; all its past habits were forgotten; every wild impulse was awake; its head erect, its nostrils dilated, its eyes flashing.

4. In another instant, before the spectators had thought of the danger, and before its friends could secure it, the fawn was bounding away through the street, and the hound in full chase. The bystanders were eager to save it; several persons immediately followed its track; the friends who had long fed and fondled it, calling the name it had hitherto known, in vain.

5. The hunter endeavored to whistle back his dog, but with no success. In half a minute the fawn had turned the first corner, dashed onward toward the lake, and thrown itself into the water. But if for a moment the startled creature believed itself safe in the cool bosom of the lake, it was soon undeceived; for the hound followed in hot and eager chase, while a dozen village dogs joined blindly in the pursuit.

6. A large crowd collected on the bank—men, women, and children—anxious for the fate of the little animal so well known to them all. Some threw themselves into boats, hoping to intercept the hound before he reached his prey. The plashing of the oars, the eager voices of men and boys, and the barking of the dogs, must have filled the heart of the poor fawn with terror and anguish,—as though every creature on the spot where it had once been caressed and fondled, had suddenly turned into a deadly foe.

7. It was soon seen that the little animal was directing its course across a bay toward the nearest borders of the forest. Immediately the owner of the hound crossed the bridge, and ran at full speed, hoping to stop his dog as he landed. On swam the fawn, as it never swam before; its delicate head scarcely seen above the water, but leaving a disturbed track, which betrayed its course alike to its friends and foes.

8. As it approached the land, the interest became intense. The hunter was already on the same side of the lake, calling loudly and angrily to his dog; but the hound seemed to have quite forgotten his master's voice in the pitiless pursuit. The fawn reached the shore. With a leap it had crossed the narrow strip of beach, and in another instant it would reach the cover of the woods.

9. The hound followed true to the scent, pointing to the same spot on the shore; his master, anxious to meet him, had run at full speed, and was now coming up at the same critical moment. Will the dog listen to his voice? or can the hunter reach him in time to seize and control him? A shout from the bank told that the fawn had passed out of sight into the forest. At the same instant, the hound, as he touched the land, felt the hunter's strong arm clutching his neck. The worst was believed to be over; the fawn was leaping up the mountain side, and its enemy was restrained. The other dogs, seeing their leader cowed, were easily managed.

10. A number of persons, men and boys, dispersed themselves through the woods in search of the little creature, but without success; they all returned to the village, reporting that the fawn had not been seen. Some thought that after its fright had passed it would return of its own accord. It wore a pretty collar with its owner's name engraved upon it, so that it could be easily known from any other fawn that might be straying about the woods.

11. Before many hours had passed, a hunter presented himself to the lady whose pet the little creature had been, and showed a collar with her name upon it. He said that he was out hunting in the morning, and saw a fawn in the distance. The little pet, instead of bounding away, as he expected, moved toward him; he took aim, fired, and shot it through the heart.

DEFINITIONS.—1. Fa̤wn, *a young deer.* Ca-rĕssed′, *fondled, petted.* 3. Dĭ-lāt′ed, *extended, spread out.* 4. Spe͡c-tā′torş, *those who look on.* 6. In-ter-çĕpt′, *to stop, to seize.* 7. Be-trāyed′, *showed.* 8. In-tĕnse′, *extreme.* 9. Sçĕnt, *track followed by the sense of smell.* Cowed, *made afraid.*

LXIV. ANNIE'S DREAM.

1. It was a clear, cold, winter evening, and all the Sinclairs but Annie had gone out for a neighborly visit. She had resolved to stay at home and study a long, difficult lesson in Natural Philosophy.

2. Left to herself, the evening passed quickly, but the lesson was learned a full half hour before the time set for the family to come home.

3. Closing her book, she leaned back in the soft armchair in which she was sitting, soon fell asleep, and began to dream. She dreamed that it was a very cold morning, and that she was standing by the dining-room stove, looking into the glass basin which was every day filled with water for evaporation.

4. "Oh, dear," she sighed, "it is nearly school-time. I don't want to go out in the cold this morning. Then there is that long lesson. I wonder if I can say it. Let me see—it takes two hundred and twelve degrees of heat, I believe, for water to evaporate—"

5. "Nonsense!" "Ridiculous!" shouted a chorus of strange little voices near by; "Look here! is this water boiling? What an idea; two hundred and twelve degrees before we can fly, ha, ha!"

6. "Who are you?" asked Annie, in amazement. "Where must I look?" "In the basin, of course."

7. Annie looked, and saw a multitude of tiny forms moving swiftly around, their numbers increasing as the heat of the fire increased. "Why you dear little things!" said she, "what are you doing down there?"

8. "We are water sprites," answered one, in the clearest voice that can be imagined, "and when this

delightful warmth comes all about us, we become so light that we fly off, as you see."

9. In another moment he had joined a crowd of his companions that were spreading their wings and flying off in curling, white clouds over Annie's head. But they were so light and thin that they soon disappeared in the air.

10. She could not see where they went, so she again turned to the basin. "Does n't it hurt you," she asked one, "to be heated—?" "Not always to two hundred and twelve," said the sprite, mischievously.

11. "No, no," replied Annie, half-vexed; "I remember, that is boiling point—but I mean, to be heated as you all are, and then to fly off in the cold?"

12. "Oh, no," laughed the little sprite; "we like it. We are made to change by God's wise laws, and so it can't hurt us. We are all the time at work, in our way, taking different shapes. It is good for us. If you will go to the window, you will find some of my brothers and sisters on the glass."

13. Annie went to the window, and at first could see nothing but some beautiful frostwork on it. Soon, however, the panes seemed to swarm with little folks. Their wings were as white as snow, and sparkled with ice jewels.

14. "Oh," cried Annie, "this is the prettiest sight I ever saw. What is your name, darling?" she asked one that wore a crown of snow roses. The little voice that replied was so sharp and fine that Annie thought it seemed like a needle point of sound, and she began to laugh.

15. "Fine Frost is our family name," it said. "I have a first name of my own, but I shall not tell you

what it is, for you are so impolite as to laugh at me."

16. "I beg your pardon, dear," said Annie; "I could not help it. I will not laugh at you any more if you will tell me how you came here. I have been talking with one of your brothers over there in the basin."

17. The little sprite then folded her wings in a dignified manner, and said, "I will tell you all I know about it, since you promise to be polite. It is a very short story, however.

18. "Last evening we all escaped from the glass basin, as you have seen our companions do this morning. Oh, how light and free we felt! But we were so very delicate and thin that no one saw us as we flew about in the air of the room.

19. "After a while I flew with these others to this window, and, as we alighted on the glass, the cold changed us from water sprites into sprites of the Fine Frost family." "It is very wonderful," said Annie. "Is it nice to be a sprite?"

20. "Oh, yes, we are very gay. All last night we had a fine time sparkling in the moonlight. I wore a long wreath full of ice pearls and diamonds. Here is a piece of it. Before long we shall be water sprites again. I see the sun is coming this way."

21. "Shall you dread to be melted?" inquired Annie. "No, indeed," answered the sprite. "I like to change my form now and then."

22. A thought flashed across Annie's brain. What if she should breathe on the frost and not wait for the sun to melt it. In a moment more she had done so. Down fell a great number of the tiny mountains and castles, carrying with them a multitude of frost

sprites, and all that could be seen was a drop of water on the window sill.

23. "Oh, dear! have I hurt them?" she exclaimed. "No, no," replied a chorus of many small voices from the drop of water, "we are only water sprites again. Nothing hurts us; we merely change." "But you are always pretty little things," said Annie. "I wish—"

24. Here a ring at the doorbell woke Annie. She started up to find the family had returned from their visit, which all declared was a delightful one. But Annie said she did not believe they had enjoyed their visit better than she had her half hour's dream.

DEFINITIONS.—1. Năt'ū-ral Phĭ-lŏs'o-phy, *the study which teaches about the laws of matter in nature.* 3. E-văp-o-rā'tion, *the act of turning into vapor.* 4. De-ḡree', *a division of space marked on an instrument such as a thermometer.* 8. Wạ'ter sprīte, *a spirit or fairy living in the water.* 10. Mĭs'chie-voŭs-ly, *in a teasing manner.* 13. Swạrm, *to be crowded.* 18. Es-ċāped', *got away, fled.*

LXV. MY GHOST.

By **Mrs. S. M. B. Piatt**, who was born near Lexington, Ky., in 1836. Among her published works may be mentioned "The Nests at Washington, and Other Poems," and "A Woman's Poems."

1. Yes, Katie, I think you are very sweet,
    Now that the tangles are out of your hair,
And you sing as well as the birds you meet,
    That are playing, like you, in the blossoms there.
But now you are coming to kiss me, you say:
    Well, what is it for? Shall I tie your shoe?
Or loop up your sleeve in a prettier way?
    "Do I know about ghosts?" Indeed I do.

2. "Have I seen one?" Yes; last evening, you know,
     We were taking a walk that you had to miss,
   (I think you were naughty, and cried to go,
     But, surely, you'll stay at home after this!)
   And, away in the twilight, lonesomely,
     ("What is the twilight?" It's—getting late!)
   I was thinking of things that were sad to me!—
     There, hush! you know nothing about them, Kate.

3. Well, we had to go through the rocky lane,
     Close to that bridge where the water roars,
   By a still, red house, where the dark and rain
     Go in when they will at the open doors.
   And the moon, that had just waked up, looked
       through
     The broken old windows, and seemed afraid,
   And the wild bats flew, and the thistles grew
     Where once in the roses the children played.

4. Just across the road by the cherry trees
     Some fallen white stones had been lying so long,
   Half hid in the grass, and under these
     There were people dead. I could hear the song
   Of a very sleepy dove as I passed
     The graveyard near, and the cricket that cried;
   And I look'd (ah! the Ghost is coming at last!)
     And something was walking at my side.

5. It seemed to be wrapped in a great dark shawl
     (For the night was a little cold, you know,);
   It would not speak. It was black and tall;
     And it walked so proudly and very slow.

Then it mocked me everything I could do:
　　Now it caught at the lightning flies like me;
Now it stopped where the elder blossoms grew;
　　Now it tore the thorns from a gray bent tree.

6. Still it followed me under the yellow moon,
　　Looking back to the graveyard now and then,
Where the winds were playing the night a tune—
　　But, Kate, a Ghost doesn't care for men,
And your papa could n't have done it harm.
　　Ah! dark-eyed darling, what is it you see?
There, you needn't hide in your dimpled arm—
　　It was only my shadow that walk'd with me!

LXVI. THE ELEPHANT.

1. The elephant is the largest of quadrupeds; his height is from eight to fourteen feet, and his length, from ten to fifteen feet. His form is that of a hog; his eyes are small and lively; his ears are long, broad and pendulous. He has two large tusks, which form the ivory of commerce, and a trunk, or proboscis, at the end of the nose, which he uses to take his food with, and for attack or defense. His color is a dark ash-brown.

2. Elephants often assemble in large troops; and, as they march in search of food, the forests seem to tremble under them. They eat the branches of trees, together with roots, herbs, leaves, grain, and fruit, but will not touch fish nor flesh. In a state of nature, they are peaceable, mild, and brave; exerting their

power only for their own protection or in defense of their own species.

3. Elephants are found both in Asia and Africa, but they are of different species, the Asiatic elephant having five toes, and the African, three. These animals are caught by stratagem, and, when tamed, they are the most gentle, obedient, and patient, as well as the most docile and sagacious of all quadrupeds. They are used to carry burdens, and for traveling. Their attachment to their masters is remarkable; and they seem to live but to serve and obey them. They always kneel to receive their riders; or the loads they have to carry.

4. The anecdotes illustrating the character of the elephant are numerous. An elephant which was kept for exhibition at London, was often required, as is usual in such exhibitions, to pick up with his trunk a piece of money thrown upon the floor for this purpose. On one occasion a sixpence was thrown, which happened to roll a little out of his reach, not far from the wall. Being desired to pick it up, he stretched out his proboscis several times to reach it; failing in this, he stood motionless a few seconds, evidently considering how to act.

5. He then stretched his proboscis in a straight line as far as he could, a little distance above the coin, and blew with great force against the wall. The angle produced by the opposition of the wall, made the current of air act under the coin, as he evidently supposed it would, and it was curious to observe the sixpence traveling toward the animal till it came within his reach, when he picked it up.

6. A soldier in India, who had frequently carried an elephant some arrack, being one day intoxicated, and

seeing himself pursued by the guard whose orders were to conduct him to prison, took refuge under the elephant. The guard soon finding his retreat, attempted in vain to take him from his asylum; for the elephant vigorously defended him with his trunk.

7. As soon as the soldier became sober, and saw himself placed under such an unwieldy animal, he was so terrified that he scarcely durst move either hand or foot; but the elephant soon caused his fears to subside by caressing him with his trunk, and thus tacitly saying, "Depart in peace."

8. A pleasing anecdote is related of an elephant which was the property of the nabob of Lucknow. There was in that city an epidemic disorder, making dreadful havoc among the inhabitants. The road to the palace gate was covered with the sick and dying, lying on the ground at the moment the nabob was about to pass.

9. Regardless of the suffering he must cause, the nabob held on his way, not caring whether his beast trod upon the poor helpless creatures or not. But the animal, more kind-hearted than his master, carefully cleared the path of the poor, helpless wretches as he went along. Some he lifted with his trunk, entirely out of the road. Some he set upon their feet, and among the others he stepped so carefully that not an individual was injured.

DEFINITIONS.—1. Quạd′rụ-ped, *an animal having four feet.* Pĕn′dū-loŭs, *hanging down.* Cŏm′merçe, *tradeᵕ.* Pro-bŏs′çis, *snout, trunk.* 3. Străt′a-ġem, *artificeᵕ.* Dŏç′ĭle, *teachableᵕ.* 6. Ar′răck, *a spirituous liquor madeᵕ from theᵕ juiceᵕ of theᵕ cocoa-nut.* A-sȳ′lum, *a refugeᵕ.* 7. Un-wiēld′y, *heavy, unmanageableᵕ.* Tăç′-it-ly, *silently.* 8. Ep-i-dĕm′ic, *affecting many peopleᵕ.* Nă′bob, *a princeᵕ in India.*

LXVII. DARE TO DO RIGHT.

Adapted from "School Days at Rugby," by Thomas Hughes, an English writer well known through this book, and its sequel, "Tom Brown at Oxford." The author was born in 1823, and died in 1896.

1. The little schoolboys went quietly to their own beds, and began undressing and talking to one another in whispers: while the elder, amongst whom was Tom, sat chatting about on one another's beds, with their jackets and waistcoats off.

2. Poor little Arthur was overwhelmed with the novelty of his position. The idea of sleeping in the room with strange boys had clearly never crossed his mind before, and was as painful as it was strange to him. He could hardly bear to take his jacket off; however, presently, with an effort, off it came, and then he paused and looked at Tom, who was sitting at the bottom of his bed, talking and laughing.

3. "Please, Brown," he whispered, "may I wash my face and hands?" "Of course, if you like," said Tom, staring: "that's your wash-hand stand under the window, second from your bed. You'll have to go down for more water in the morning if you use it all."

4. And on he went with his talk, while Arthur stole timidly from between the beds out to his wash-hand stand, and began his ablutions, thereby drawing for a moment on himself the attention of the room.

5. On went the talk and laughter. Arthur finished his washing and undressing, and put on his night-gown. He then looked round more nervously than ever. Two or three of the little boys were already in bed, sitting up with their chins on their knees. The light burned clear, the noise went on.

6. It was a trying moment for the poor, little, lonely boy; however, this time he did not ask Tom what he might or might not do, but dropped all his knees by his bedside, as he had done every day from his childhood, to open his heart to Him who heareth the cry and beareth the sorrows of the tender child, and the strong man in agony.

7. Tom was sitting at the bottom of his bed unlacing his boots, so that his back was towards Arthur, and he did not see what had happened, and looked up in wonder at the sudden silence. Then two or three boys laughed and sneered, and a big, brutal fellow, who was standing in the middle of the room, picked up a slipper and shied it at the kneeling boy, calling him a sniveling young shaver.

8. Then Tom saw the whole, and the next moment the boot he had just pulled off flew straight at the head of the bully, who had just time to throw up his arm and catch it on his elbow. "Confound you, Brown; what's that for?" roared he, stamping with pain. "Never mind what I mean," said Tom, stepping on to the floor, every drop of blood in his body tingling: "if any fellow wants the other boot, he knows how to get it."

9. What would have been the result is doubtful, for at this moment the sixth-form boy came in, and not another word could be said. Tom and the rest rushed into bed and finished their unrobing there, and the old janitor had put out the candle in another minute, and toddled on to the next room, shutting the door with his usual, "Good night, gen'l'm'n."

10. There were many boys in the room by whom that little scene was taken to heart before they slept. But sleep seemed to have deserted the pillow of poor

Tom. For some time his excitement and the flood of
memories which chased one another though his brain,
kept him from thinking or resolving. His head
throbbed, his heart leapt, and he could hardly keep
himself from springing out of bed and rushing about
the room.

11. Then the thought of his own mother came across hime, and the promise he had made at her knee, years ago, never to forget to kneel by his bedside and give himself up to his Father before he laid his head on the pillow, from which it might never rise; and he lay down gently, and cried as if his heart would break. He was only fourteen years old.

DEFINITIONS.—1. Wāist′cōat, *a vest.* 2. O-ver-whĕlmed′, *over-come, cast down.* 3. Nŏv′el-ty, *newness.* 4. Ab-lū′tion, *the act of washing.* 7. Sneered, *showed contempt.* 8. Bŭl′ly, *a noisy, blustering fellow, more insolent than courageous.* Tĭn′gling, *having a thrilling feeling.*

NOTES.—"Rugby," the scene of this story, is a celebrated grammar school which was established at the town of Rugby, England, in 1567.

9. *Sixth-form boy.* The school was graded into six classes or "forms," and the boys of the highest, or sixth, form were expected to keep the smaller boys under them in order.

EXERCISES.—What were Arthur's feelings the first night at Rugby? Relate what happened when he said his prayers. What do you think of the boy who threw the slipper? Was Tom right in defending Arthur from insult?

LXVIII. DARE TO DO RIGHT.

(CONCLUDED.)

1. It was no light act of courage in those days for a little fellow to say his prayers publicly, even at Rugby. A few years later, when Arnold's manly piety had begun to leaven the school, the tables turned: before he died, in the Schoolhouse at least,

and I believe in the other houses, the rule was the other way.

2. But poor Tom had come to school in other times. The first few nights after he came he did not kneel down because of the noise, but sat up in bed till the candle was out, and then stole out and said his prayers, in fear lest some one should find him out. So did many another poor little fellow.

3. Then he began to think that he might just as well say his prayers in bed, and then that it did not matter whether he was kneeling, or sitting, or lying down. And so it had come to pass with Tom, as with all who will not confess their Lord before men; and for the last year he had probably not said his prayers in earnest a dozen times.

4. Poor Tom! the first and bitterest feeling, which was like to break his heart, was the sense of his own cowardice. The vice of all others which he loathed was brought in and burned in on his own soul. He had lied to his mother, to his conscience, to his God. How could he bear it? And then the poor, little, weak boy, whom he had pitied and almost scorned for his weakness, had done that which he, braggart as he was, dared not do.

5. The first dawn of comfort came to him in vowing to himself that he would stand by that boy through thick and thin, and cheer him, and help him, and bear his burdens, for the good deed done that night. Then he resolved to write home next day and tell his mother all, and what a coward her son had been. And then peace came to him as he resolved, lastly, to bear his testimony next morning.

6. The morning would be harder than the night to begin with, but he felt that he could not afford to let

one chance slip. Several times he faltered, for the Devil showed him, first, all his old friends calling him "Saint," and "Squaretoes" and a dozen hard names, and whispered to him that his motives would be misunderstood, and he would be left alone with the new boy; whereas, it was his duty to keep all means of influence, that he might do good to the largest number.

7. And then came the more subtle temptation, "shall I not be showing myself braver than others by doing this? Have I any right to begin it now? Ought I not rather to pray in my own study, letting other boys know that I do so, and trying to lead them to it, while in public, at least, I should go on as I have done?" However, his good angel was too strong that night, and he turned on his side and slept, tired of trying to reason, but resolved to follow the impulse which had been so strong, and in which he had found peace.

8. Next morning he was up and washed and dressed, all but his jacket and waistcoat, just as the ten minutes' bell began to ring, and then in the face of the whole room he knelt down to pray. Not five words could he say,—the bell mocked him; he was listening for every whisper in the room,—what were they all thinking of him?

9. He was ashamed to go on kneeling, ashamed to rise from his knees. At last, as it were from his inmost heart, a still, small voice seemed to breathe forth the words of the publican, "God be merciful to me a sinner!" He repeated them over and over, clinging to them as for his life, and rose from his knees comforted and humbled, and ready to face the whole world.

10. It was not needed: two other boys besides Arthur had already followed his example, and he went down to the great school with a glimmering of another lesson in his heart,—the lesson that he who has conquered his own coward spirit has conquered the whole outward world; and that other one which the old prophet learned in the cave at Mount Horeb, when he hid his face, and the still, small voice asked, "What doest thou here, Elijah?"—that however we may fancy ourselves alone on the side of good, the King and Lord of men is nowhere without his witnesses; for in every society, however seemingly corrupt and godless, there are those who have not bowed the knee to Baal.

11. He found, too, how greatly he had exaggerated the effect to be produced by his act. For a few nights there was a sneer or a laugh when he knelt down, but this passed off soon, and one by one all the other boys but three or four followed the lead.

DEFINITIONS.—1. Lĕav'en, *to make a general change, to imbue.* 4. Lōathed, *hated, detested.* Brăg'gart, *a boaster.* 5. Vow'ing, *making a solemn promise to God.* Tĕs'ti-mo-ny, *open declaration.* 6. Făl'tered, *hesitated.* Mō'tĭve, *that which causes action, cause, reason.* 7. Sŭb'tle (pro. sŭt'l), *artful, cunning.* Stŭd'y, *a private room devoted to study.* 10. Glĭm'mer-ing, *a faint view.*

NOTES.—1. *Arnold's.* Dr. Thomas Arnold was head master at Rugby nearly fifteen years. His influence on the character of the boys was very marked, and soon made the school celebrated throughout England.

The Schoolhouse was the name of one of the numerous buildings belonging to Rugby.

EXERCISES.—Relate Tom's early experience at Rugby. Was it courageous in him to stop saying his prayers? How did he feel over it? What did he resolve to do? Did he carry out his resolve? What two lessons was he taught?

LXIX. THE WRECK OF THE HESPERUS.

By **Henry Wadsworth Longfellow,** one of the greatest of American poets. He was born in Portland, Me., in 1807. For some years he held the professorship of Modern Languages in Bowdoin College, and later a similar professorship in Harvard College. He died March 24th, 1882.

1. It was the schooner Hesperus,
   That sailed the wintry sea;
   And the skipper had taken his little daughter,
   To bear him company.

2. Blue were her eyes as the fairy flax,
   Her checks like the dawn of day,
   And her bosom white as the hawthorn buds,
   That ope in the month of May.

3. The skipper, he stood beside the helm,
   His pipe was in his mouth,
   And he watched how the veering flaw did blow
   The smoke now west, now south.

4. Then up and spake an old sailor,
   Had sailed to the Spanish Main,
   "I pray thee, put into yonder port,
   For I fear the hurricane.

5. "Last night, the moon had a golden ring,
   And to-night no moon we see!"
   The skipper, he blew a whiff from his pipe,
   And a scornful laugh laughed he.

6. Colder and louder blew the wind,
   A gale from the northeast;
   The snow fell hissing in the brine,
   And the billows frothed like yeast.

7. Down came the storm, and smote amain
    The vessel in its strength;
  She shuddered and paused, like a frighted steed,
    Then leaped her cable's length.

8. "Come hither! come hither! my little daughter,
    And do not tremble so;
  For I can weather the roughest gale
    That ever wind did blow."

9. He wrapped her warm in his seaman's coat,
    Against the stinging blast:
  He cut a rope from a broken spar,
    And bound her to the mast.

10. "O father! I hear the church bells ring,
    Oh say, what may it be?"
  "'Tis a fog bell on a rock-bound coast!"
  And he steered for the open sea.

11. "O father! I hear the sound of guns,
    Oh say, what may it be?"
  "Some ship in distress, that can not live
    In such an angry sea!"

12. "O father! I see a gleaming light,
    Oh say, what may it be?"
  But the father answered never a word,
    A frozen corpse was he.

13. Lashed to the helm, all stiff and stark,
    With his face turned to the skies,
  The lantern gleamed through the gleaming snow
    On his fixed and glassy eyes.

14. Then the maiden clasped her hands, and prayed
    That saved she might be;
  And she thought of Christ, who stilled the wave
    On the lake of Galilee.

15. And fast through the midnight dark and drear,
    Through the whistling sleet and snow,
  Like a sheeted ghost, the vessel swept
    Tow'rds the reef of Norman's Woe.

16. And ever the fitful gusts between
    A sound came from the land:
  It was the sound of the trampling surf
    On the rocks and the hard sea sand.

17. The breakers were right beneath her bows,
    She drifted a dreary wreck,
  And a whooping billow swept the crew
    Like icicles from her deck.

18. She struck where the white and fleecy waves
    Looked soft as carded wool,
  But the cruel rocks, they gored her side
    Like the horns of an angry bull.

19. Her rattling shrouds, all sheathed in ice,
    With the masts, went by the board;
  Like a vessel of glass, she stove and sank,
    Ho! ho! the breakers roared!

20. At day break, on the bleak seabeach,
    A fisherman stood aghast,
  To see the form of a maiden fair
    Lashed close to a drifting mast.

21. The salt sea was frozen on her breast,
　　The salt tears in her eyes;
　And he saw her hair, like the brown seaweed,
　　On the billows fall and rise.
22. Such was the wreck of the Hesperus
　　In the midnight and the snow:
　Heav'n save us all from a death like this
　　On the reef of Norman's Woe!

DEFINITIONS.—1. Skĭp´per, *the master of a small merchant vessel.* 3. Veer´ing, *changing.* Flăw, *a sudden gust of wind.* 4. Pōrt, *harbor.* 6. Brīne, *the sea.* 7. A-māin´, *with sudden force.* 8. Wĕath´er, *to endure, to resist.* 9. Spär, *a long beam.* 13. Hĕlm, *the instrument by which a ship is steered.* 18. Cärd´ed, *cleaned by combing.* 19. Shroudṣ, *sets of ropes reaching from the mastheads to the sides of a vessel to support the masts.* Stōve, *broke in.*

NOTES.—This piece is written in the style of the old English ballads. The syllables marked (´) have a peculiar accent not usually allowed.

4. The Spanish Main was the name formerly applied to the northern coast of South America from the Mosquito Territory to the Leeward Islands.

15. The reef of Norman's Woe. A dangerous ledge of rocks on the Massachusetts coast, near Gloucester harbor.

19. Went by the board. A sailor's expression, meaning "fell over the side of the vessel."

LXX. ANECDOTES OF BIRDS.

1. I had once a favorite black hen, "a great beauty," as she was called by everyone, and so I thought her; her feathers were so jetty, and her topping so white and full! She knew my voice as well as any dog, and used to run cackling and bustling to

my hand to receive the fragments that I never failed to collect from the breakfast table for "Yarico," as she was called.

2. Yarico, by the time she was a year old, hatched a respectable family of chickens; little, cowering, timid things at first, but, in due time, they became fine chubby ones; and old Norah said, "If I could only keep Yarico out of the copse, it would do; but the copse is full of weasels and of foxes.

3. "I have driven her back twenty times; but she watches till some one goes out of the gate, and then she's off again. It is always the case with young hens, Miss; they think they know better than their keepers; and nothing cures them but losing a brood or two of chickens." I have often thought since that young people, as well as young hens, buy their experience equally dear.

4. One morning; after breakfast, I went to seek my favorite in the poultry yard; plenty of hens were there, but no Yarico. The gate was open, and, as I concluded she had sought the forbidden copse, I proceeded there, accompanied by the yard mastiff; a noble fellow, steady and sagacious as a judge.

5. At the end of a lane, flanked on one side by a quickset hedge, on the other by a wild common, what was called the copse commenced; but before I arrived near the spot I heard a loud and tremendous cackling, and met two young, long-legged pullets, running with both wings and feet toward home. Jock pricked up his sharp ears, and would have set off at full gallop to the copse; but I restrained him, hastening onward, however, at the top of my speed, thinking I had as good a right to see what was the matter as Jock.

6. Poor Yarico! An impertinent fox cub had at-

tempted to carry off one of her children; but she had managed to get them behind her in the hedge, and venturing boldly forth had placed herself in front, and positively kept the impudent animal at bay. His desire for plunder had prevented his noticing our approach, and Jock soon made him feel the superiority of an English mastiff over a cub fox.

7. The most interesting portion of my tale is to come. Yarico not only never afterward ventured to the copse, but formed a strong friendship for the dog which had preserved her family. Whenever he appeared in the yard, she would run to meet him, prating and clucking all the time, and impeding his progress by walking between his legs, to his no small annoyance. If any other dog entered the yard, she would fly at him most furiously, thinking, perhaps, that he would injure her chickens; but she evidently considered Jock her especial protector, and treated him accordingly.

8. It was very droll to see the peculiar look with which he regarded his feathered friend; not knowing exactly what to make of her civilities, and doubting how they should be received. When her family were educated, and able to do without her care, she was a frequent visitor at Jock's kennel, and would, if permitted, roost there at night, instead of returning with the rest of the poultry to the henhouse. Yarico certainly was a most grateful and interesting bird. * *

9. One could almost believe a parrot had intellect, when he keeps up a conversation so spiritedly; and it is certainly singular to observe how accurately a well-trained bird will apply his knowledge. A friend of mine knew one that had been taught many sentences; thus, "Sally, Poll wants her breakfast!" "Sally,

Poll wants her tea!" but she never mistook the one for the other; breakfast was invariably demanded in the morning, and tea in the afternoon; and she always hailed her master, but no one else, by "How do you do, Mr. A?"

10. She was a most amusing bird, and could whistle dogs, which she had great pleasure in doing. She would drop bread out of her cage as she hung at the street door, and whistle a number about her, and then, just as they were going to possess themselves of her bounty, utter a shrill scream of "Get out, dogs!" with such vehemence and authority as dispersed the assembled company without a morsel, to her infinite delight. * * *

11. How wonderful is that instinct by which the bird of passage performs its annual migration! But how still more wonderful is it when the bird, after its voyage of thousands of miles has been performed, and new lands visited, returns to the precise window or eaves where, the summer before, it first enjoyed existence! And yet, such is unquestionably the fact.

12. Four brothers had watched with indignation the felonious attempts of a sparrow to possess himself of the nest of a house martin, in which lay its young brood of four unfledged birds.

13. The little fellows considered themselves as champions for the bird which had come over land and sea, and chosen its shelter under their mother's roof. They therefore marshaled themselves with blowguns, to execute summary vengeance; but their well-meant endeavors brought destruction upon the mud-built domicile they wished to defend. Their artillery loosened the foundations, and down it came, precipitating its four little inmates to the ground. The mother of the

children, Good Samaritan-like, replaced the little out-casts in their nest, and set it in the open window of an unoccupied chamber.

14. The parent birds, after the first terror was over, did not appear disconcerted by the change of situation, but hourly fed their young as usual, and testified, by their unwearied twitter of pleasure, the satisfaction and confidence they felt. There the young birds were duly fledged, and from that window they began their flight, and entered upon life.

15. The next spring, with the reappearance of the martins, came four, which familiarly flew into the chamber, visited all the walls, and expressed their recognition by the most clamorous twitterings of joy. They were, without question, the very birds that had been bred there the preceding year.

DEFINITIONS.—2. Cŏpse, *a grove of small trees or bushes.* 4. Sa-ḡā′ciŏŭs, *quick in discernment.* 6. Im-pẽr′ti-nent, *rude, intrusive.* 8. Kĕn′nel, *a place for dogs.* 10. Vē′he-mençe, *force.* 11. Mī-ḡrā′tion, *change of place, removal.* 12. Fe-lō′ni-oŭs, *criminal.* 13. Dŏm′i-çile, *the home or residence of anyone.* Ar-tĭl′er-y, *weapons of warfare.* 14. Dĭs-con-çẽrt′ed, *interrupted, confused.* 15. Rĕc-oḡ-nĭ′tion, *recollection of a former acquaintance.*

LXXI. THE RAINBOW PILGRIMAGE.

By **Sara J. Lippincott**, born at Onondaga, N. Y., in 1823, of New England parentage. Under the name of "Grace Greenwood" she has written many charming stories for children. Some of her best sketches are in "Records of Five Years."

1. One summer afternoon, when I was about eight years of age, I was standing at an eastern window, looking at a beautiful rainbow that, bending from the

sky, seemed to be losing itself in a thick, swampy wood about a quarter of a mile distant.

2. It happened that no one was in the room with me then but my brother Rufus, who was just recovering from a severe illness, and was sitting, propped up with pillows, in an easy-chair, looking out, with me, at the rainbow.

3. "See, brother," I said, "it drops right down among the cedars, where we go in the spring to find winter-greens!"

4. "Do you know, Gracie," said my brother, with a very serious face, "that if you should go to the end of the rain how, you would find there purses filled with money, and great pots of gold and silver?"

5. "Is it truly so?" I asked.

6. "Truly so," answered my brother, with a smile. Now, I was a simple-hearted child who believed everything that was told me, although I was again and again imposed upon; so, without another word, I darted out of the door, and set forth toward the wood. My brother called after me as loudly as he was able, but I did not heed him.

7. I cared nothing for the wet grass, which was sadly drabbling my clean frock,—on and on I ran: I was so sure that I knew just where that rainbow ended. I remember how glad and proud I was in my thoughts, and what fine presents I promised to all my friends out of my great riches.

8. So thinking, and laying delightful plans, almost before I knew it I had reached the cedar grove, and the end of the rainbow was not there! But I saw it shining down among the trees a little farther off; so on and on I struggled, through the thick bushes and over logs, till I came within the sound of a stream

which ran through the swamp. Then I thought, "What if the rainbow should come down right in the middle of that deep, muddy brook!"

9. Ah! but I was frightened for my heavy pots of gold and silver, and my purses of money. How should I ever find them there? and what a time I should have getting them out! I reached the bank of the stream, and "the end was not yet." But I could see it a little way off on the other side. I crossed the creek on a fallen tree, and still ran on, though my limbs seemed to give way, and my side ached with fatigue.

10. The woods grew thicker and darker, the ground more wet and swampy, and I found, as many grown people had found before me, that there was rather hard traveling in a journey after, riches. Suddenly I met in my way a large porcupine, who made himself still larger when he saw me, as a cross cat raises its back and makes tails at a dog. Fearing that he would shoot his sharp quills at me, I ran from him as fast as my tired feet would carry me.

11. In my fright and hurry I forgot to keep my eye on the rainbow, as I had done before; and when, at last, I remembered and looked for it, it was nowhere in sight! It had quite faded away. When I saw that it was indeed gone, I burst into tears; for I had lost all my treasures, and had nothing to show for my pilgrimage but muddy feet and a wet and torn frock. So I set out for home.

12. But I soon found that my troubles had only begun; I could not find my way: I was lost! I could not tell which was east or west, north or south, but wandered about here and there, crying and calling, though I knew that no one could hear me.

13. All at once I heard voices shouting and hallooing; but, instead of being rejoiced at this, I was frightened, fearing that the Indians were upon me! I crawled under some bushes, by the side of a large log, and lay perfectly still. I was wet, cold, scared,— altogether very miserable indeed; yet, when the voices came near, I did not start up and show myself.

14. At last I heard my own name called; but I remembered that Indians were very cunning, and thought they might have found it out some way, so I did not answer. Then came a voice near me, that sounded like that of my eldest brother, who lived away from home, and whom I had not seen for many months; but I dared not believe that the voice was his.

15. Soon some one sprang up on the log by which I lay, and stood there calling. I could not see his face; I could only see the tips of his toes, but by them I saw that he wore a nice pair of boots, and not moccasins. Yet I remembered that some Indians dressed like white folks; so I still kept quiet, till I heard shouted over me a pet name, which this brother had given me. It was the funniest name in the world.

16. I knew that no Indian knew of the name, as it was a little family secret; so I sprang up, and caught my brother about the ankles. I hardly think that an Indian could have given a louder yell than he gave then; and he jumped so that he fell off the log down by my side. But nobody was hurt; and, after kissing me till he had kissed away all my tears, he hoisted me on to his shoulder, called my other brothers, who were hunting in different directions, and we all set out for home.

17. I had been gone nearly three hours, and had wandered a number of miles. My brother Joseph's coming and asking for me, had first set them to inquiring and searching me out. When I went into the room where my brother Rufus sat, he said, "Why, my poor little sister! I did not mean to send you off on such a wild-goose chase to the end of the rainbow. I thought you would know I was only quizzing you."

18. Then my eldest brother took me on his knee, and told me what the rainbow really is: that it was only painted air, and does not rest on the earth, so nobody could ever find the end; and that God has set it in the cloud to remind him and us of his promise never again to drown the world with a flood. "Oh, I think God's Promise would be a beautiful name for the rainbow!" I said.

19. "Yes," replied my mother, "but it tells us something more than that he will not send great floods upon the earth,—it tells us of his beautiful love always bending over us from the skies. And I trust that when my little girl sets forth on a pil-grim=age to find God's love, she will be led by the rainbow of his promise through all the dark places of this world to 'treasures laid up in heaven,' better, far better, than silver or gold."

DEFINITIONS.—2. Re-cŏv'er-ing, *growing well.* 3. Wĭn'ter—ġreen, *a creeping evergreen plant with bright red berries.* 6. Im—pōṣed', (used with *on* or *upon*), *deceived, misled.* 7. Drăb'-bling, *making dirty by drawing in mud and water.* 10. Pôr'cu-pīne, *a small quadruped whose body is covered with sharp quills.* 11. Pĭl'ġrim-aġe, *journey.* 15. Mŏc'ca-sinṣ, *shoes of deerskin without soles, such as are usually worn by Indians.* 17. Quĭz'zing, *making sport of.*

LXXII. THE OLD OAKEN BUCKET.

By **Samuel Woodworth**, who was born in Massachusetts in 1785. He was both author and editor. This is his best known poem.

1. How dear to this heart are the scenes of my childhood,
   When fond recollection presents them to view!
   The orchard, the meadow, the deep tangled wildwood,
   And every loved spot which my infancy knew;

The wide-spreading pond, and the mill that stood by it:
　　The bridge and the rock where the cataract fell:
The cot of my father, the dairy house nigh it,
　　And e'en the rude bucket which hung in the well:
The old oaken bucket, the ironbound bucket,
　　The moss-covered bucket which hung in the well.

2. That moss-covered vessel I hail as a treasure;
　　For often, at noon, when returned from the field,
I found it the source of an exquisite pleasure,
　　The purest and sweetest that nature can yield.
How ardent I seized it, with hands that were glowing,
　　And quick to the white-pebble bottom it fell;
Then soon, with the emblem of truth overflowing,
　　And dripping with coolness, it rose from the well:
The old oaken bucket, the ironbound bucket,
　　The moss-covered bucket arose from the well.

3. How sweet from the green mossy brim to receive it,
　　As poised on the curb, it inclined to my lips!
Not a full blushing goblet could tempt me to leave it,
　　Though filled with the nectar which Jupiter sips;
And now, far removed from thy loved situation,
　　The tear of regret will intrusively swell,
As fancy reverts to my father's plantation,
　　And sighs for the bucket which hangs in the well:
The old oaken bucket, the ironbound bucket,
　　The moss-covered bucket, which hangs in the well.

DEFINITIONS.—1. Căt'a-răet, *a great fall of water.* 2. O-ver-flōw'ing, *running over.* Ex'qui-şite, *exceeding, extreme.* 3. Poişed', *balanced.* Gŏblet, *a kind of cup or drinking vessel.* Nĕe'-tar, *the drink of the gods.* In-tru'sĭve-ly, *without right or welcome.* Re-vērts', *returns.*

EXERCISES.—Who was the author of "The Old Oaken Bucket"? What is said of this piece? What does the poem describe? and what feeling does it express?

LXXIII. THE SERMON ON THE MOUNT.

1. And seeing the multitudes, he went up into a mountain: and when he was set, his disciples came unto him; and he opened his mouth and taught them, saying,

2. Blessed are the poor in spirit; for theirs is the kingdom of heaven. Blessed are they that mourn; for they shall be comforted. Blessed are the meek; for they shall inherit the earth.

3. Blessed are they which do hunger and thirst after righteousness; for they shall be filled. Blessed are the merciful; for they shall obtain mercy. Blessed are the pure in heart; for they shall see God.

4. Blessed are the peacemakers; for they shall be called the children of God. Blessed are they which are persecuted for righteousness' sake; for theirs is the kingdom of heaven.

5. Blessed are ye when men shall revile you, and persecute you, and shall say all manner of evil against you falsely, for my sake. Rejoice and be exceeding glad; for great is your reward in heaven. * * *

6. Ye have heard that it hath been said by them of old time, Thou shalt not forswear thyself, but shalt perform unto the Lord thine oaths: but I say unto you, Swear not at all; neither by heaven; for it is God's throne: nor by the earth; for it is his footstool: neither by Jerusalem; for it is the city of the great King.

7. Neither shalt thou swear by thy head, because thou canst not make one hair white or black. But let your communication be, Yea, yea; Nay, nay: for whatsoever is more than these cometh of evil.

8. Ye have heard that it hath been said, An eye for an eye, and a tooth for a tooth: but I say unto you, That ye resist not evil; but whosoever shall smite thee on thy right cheek, turn to him the other also. And if any man will sue thee at the law, and take away thy coat, let him have thy cloak also. And whosoever shall compel thee to go a mile, go with him twain. Give to him that asketh thee, and from him that would borrow of thee turn not thou away.

9. Ye have heard that it hath been said, Thou shalt love thy neighbor and hate thine enemy: but I say unto you, Love your enemies; bless them that curse you, do good to them that hate you, and pray for them which despitefully use you and persecute you; that ye may be the children of your Father which is in heaven: for he maketh his sun to rise on the evil and on the good, and sendeth rain on the just and on the unjust.

10. For if ye love them which love you, what reward have ye? do not even the publicans the same? And if ye salute your brethren only, what do ye more than others? do not even the publicans so? Be ye, therefore, perfect, even as your Father which is in heaven is perfect. * * *

11. Judge not, that ye be not judged. For with what judgment ye judge, ye shall be judged: and with what measure ye mete, it shall be measured to you again. And why beholdest thou the mote that is in thy brother's eye, but considerest not the beam that is in thine own eye?

12. Or how wilt thou say to thy brother, Let me pull out the mote out of thine eye; and, behold, a beam is in thine own eye? Thou hypocrite, first cast

out the beam out of thine own eye; and then shalt thou see clearly to cast out the mote out of thy brother's eye. * * *

13. Ask, and it shall be given you; seek, and ye shall find; knock, and it shall be opened unto you: for everyone that asketh, receiveth; and he that seeketh, findeth; and to him that knocketh, it shall be opened. Or what man is there of you, whom if his son ask bread, will he give him a stone? Or if he ask a fish, will he give him a serpent?

14. If ye then, being evil, know how to give good gifts unto your children, how much more shall your Father which is in heaven give good things to them that ask him? Therefore all things whatsoever ye would that men should do to you, do ye even so to them; for this is the law and the prophets. * * *

15. Whosoever heareth these sayings of mine, and doeth them, I will liken him unto a wise man, which built his house upon a rock: and the rain descended, and the floods came, and the winds blew, and beat upon that house; and it fell not; for it was founded upon a rock.

16. And everyone that heareth these sayings of mine, and doeth them not, shall be likened unto a foolish man, which built his house upon the sand: and the rain descended, and the floods came, and the winds blew, and beat upon that house; and it fell: and great was the fall of it.

17. And it came to pass, when Jesus had ended these sayings, the people were astonished at his doctrine: for he taught them as one having authority, and not as the scribes.

DEFINITIONS.—1. Dis-çï'ple, *one who receives instruction from another.* 2. Blĕss'ed, *happy.* In-hĕr'it, *to come into possession of.*

5. Re-vīle′, *to speak against without cause*. Pĕr′se-cūte, *to punish on account of religion.* 6. *For-swear′, to swear falsely.* 9. De-spīte′ful-ly, *maliciously, cruelly.* 10. Pŭb′li-eanṣ, *tax collectors* (they were often oppressive and were hated by the Jews). 11. Mēte, *to measure.* Mōte, *a small particle.* 12. Hўp′o-erīte, *a false pretender.* 17. Seribeṣ, *men among the Jews who read and explained the law to the people.*

EXERCISES.—Who delivered this sermon? Who are blessed? and why? Is it right to swear? How should we treat our enemies? Should we judge others harshly? What does Jesus say of him who finds faults in his neighbor, but does not see his own? What is said about prayer? About our conduct to others?

LXXIV. THE YOUNG WITNESS.

By S. H. HAMMOND.

1. A little girl nine years of age was brought into court, and offered as a witness against a prisoner who was on trial for a crime committed in her father's house.

2. "Now, Emily," said the counsel for the prisoner, "I wish to know if you understand the nature of an oath?"

3. "I don't know what you mean," was the simple answer.

4. "Your Honor," said the counsel, addressing the judge, "it is evident that this witness should be rejected. She does not understand the nature of an oath."

5. "Let us see," said the judge. "Come here, my daughter."

6. Assured by the kind tone and manner of the judge, the child stepped toward him, and looked con-

fidingly in his face, with a calm, clear eye, and in a manner so artless and frank that it went straight to the heart.

7. "Did you ever take an oath?" inquired the judge.

8. The little girl stepped back with a look of horror; and the red blood rose and spread in a blush all over her face and neck, as she answered, "No, sir." She thought he intended to ask if she had ever used profane language.

9. "I do not mean that," said the judge, who saw her mistake; "I mean were you ever a witness?"

10. "No, sir; I never was in court before," was the answer.

11. He handed her the Bible open. "Do you know that book, my daughter?"

12. She looked at it and answered, "Yes, sir; it is the Bible."

13. "Do you ever read in it?" he asked.

14. "Yes, sir; every evening."

15. "Can you tell me what the Bible is?" inquired the judge.

16. "It is the word of the great God," she answered.

17. "Well," said the judge, "place your hand upon this Bible, and listen to what I say;" and he repeated slowly and solemnly the following oath: "Do you swear that in the evidence which you shall give in this case, you will tell the truth, and nothing but the truth; and that you will ask God to help you?"

18. "I do," she replied.

19. "Now," said the judge, "you have been sworn as a witness; will you tell me what will befall you if you do not tell the truth?"

20. "I shall be shut up in the state prison," answered the child.

21. "Anything else?" asked the judge.

22. "I shall never go to heaven," she replied.

23. "How do you know this?" asked the judge again.

24. The child took the Bible, turned rapidly to the chapter containing the commandments, and, pointing to the one which reads, "Thou shalt not bear false witness against thy neighbor," said, "I learned that before I could read."

25. "Has anyone talked with you about being a witness in court here against this man?" inquired the judge.

26. "Yes, sir," she replied, "my mother heard they wanted me to be a witness; and last night she called me to her room, and asked me to tell her the Ten Commandments; and then we kneeled down together, and she prayed that I might understand how wicked it was to bear false witness against my neighbor, and that God would help me, a little child, to tell the truth as it was before him.

27. "And when I came up here with father, she kissed me, and told me to remember the Ninth Commandment, and that God would hear every word that I said."

28. "Do you believe this?" asked the judge, while a tear glistened in his eye, and his lip quivered with emotion.

29. "Yes, sir," said the child, with a voice and manner which showed that her conviction of the truth was perfect.

30. "God bless you, my child," said the judge, "you have a good mother. The witness is compe-

tent," he continued. "Were I on trial for my life, and innocent of the charge against me, I would pray God for such a witness as this. Let her be examined."

31. She told her story with the simplicity of a child, as she was; but her voice and manner carried conviction of her truthfulness to every heart.

32. The lawyers asked her many perplexing questions, but she did not vary in the least from her first statement.

33. The truth, as spoken by a little child, was sublime. Falsehood and perjury had preceded her testimony; but before her testimony, falsehood was scattered like chaff.

34. The little child, for whom a mother had prayed for strength to be given her to speak the truth as it was before God, broke the cunning device of matured villainy to pieces, like a potter's vessel. The strength that her mother prayed for was given her; and the sublime and terrible simplicity,—terrible to the prisoner and his associates,—was like a revelation from God himself.

DEFINITIONS.—1. Wĭt′ness, *one who gives testimony.* Commĭt′ted, *done, performed.* 2. Coun′sel, *a lawyer.* 4. Re-jĕet′ed, *refused.* 6. As-sụred′, *made bold.* Con-fīd′ing-ly, *with trust.* 8. Pro-fāne′, *irreverent, taking the name of God in vain.* 33. Pēr′ju-ry, *the act of willfully making a false oath.* Chȧff, *the light dry husk of grains or grasses.* 34. Ma-tūred′, *perfected, fully developed.* Pŏt′ter, *one whose occupation is to make earthen vessels.* Rĕv-e-lā′tion, *the act of disclosing or showing what was before unknown.*

EXERCISES.—What is this story about? Why did the counsel wish to have Emily refused as a witness? Was she a fit person to be a witness? How was this shown? Which commandment forbids us to bear false witness? What was the result of Emily's testimony?

LXXV. KING SOLOMON AND THE ANTS.

By **John Greenleaf Whittier**, born near Haverhill, Mass., In 1807, and died at Hampton Falls, N. H., In 1892. Until he was eighteen years old he worked on the farm, and during that time learned the trade at a shoe-maker. He afterwards became an editor and one of the first poets of America.

1. Out from Jerusalem
   The king rode with his great
   War chiefs and lords of state,
And Sheba's queen with them.

2. Proud in the Syrian sun,
   In gold and purple sheen,
   The dusky Ethiop queen
Smiled on King Solomon.

3. Wisest of men, he knew
   The languages of all
   The creatures great or small
That trod the earth or flew.

4. Across an ant-hill led
   The king's path, and he heard
   Its small folk, and their word
He thus interpreted:

5. "Here comes the king men greet
   As wise and good and just,
   To crush us in the dust
Under his heedless feet."

6. The great king bowed his head,
   And saw the wide surprise
   Of the Queen of Sheba's eyes
As he told her what they said.

7. "O king!" she whispered sweet,
   "Too happy fate have they
   Who perish in thy way
   Beneath thy gracious feet!

8. "Thou of the God-lent crown,
   Shall these vile creatures dare
   Murmur against thee where
   The knees of kings kneel down?"

9. "Nay," Solomon replied,
   "The wise and strong should seek
   The welfare of the weak;"
   And turned his horse aside.

10. His train, with quick alarm,
    Curved with their leader round
    The ant-hill's peopled mound,
    And left it free from harm.

11. The jeweled head bent low;
    "O king!" she said, "henceforth
    The secret of thy worth
    And wisdom well I know.

12. "Happy must be the State
    Whose ruler heedeth more
    The murmurs of the poor
    Than flatteries of the great."

DEFINITIONS.—4. In-tĕr′pret-ed, *explained the meaning of.*
5. Greet, *address, salute.* 9. Wĕl′fâre, *happiness.* 10. Trāin, *a body of followers.* 12. Flăt′ter-ies, *praises for the purpose of gratifying vanity or gaining favor.*

LXXVI. RIVERMOUTH THEATER.

From "The Story of a Bad Boy," by **Thomas Bailey Aldrich**. The author was born at Portsmouth, N. H., in 1836. When quite young his family moved to Louisiana, but he was sent back to New England to be educated, and later he located at New York. He is a well-known writer of both prose and poetry.

1. "Now, boys, what shall we do?" I asked, addressing a thoughtful conclave of seven, assembled in our barn one dismal, rainy afternoon. "Let's have a theater," suggested Binny Wallace.

2. The very thing! But where? The loft of the stable was ready to burst with hay provided for Gypsy, but the long room over the carriage house was unoccupied. The place of all places! My managerial eye saw at a glance its capabilities for a theater.

3. I had been to the play a great many times in New Orleans, and was wise in matters pertaining to the drama. So here, in due time, was set up some extraordinary scenery of my own painting. The curtain, I recollect, though it worked smoothly enough on other occasions, invariably hitched during the performances.

4. The theater, however, was a success, as far as it went. I retired from the business with no fewer than fifteen hundred pins, after deducting the headless, the pointless, and the crooked pins with which our doorkeeper frequently got "stuck." From first to last we took in a great deal of this counterfeit money. The price of admission to the "Rivermouth Theater" was twenty pins. I played all the principal characters myself—not that I was a finer actor than the other boys, but because I owned the establishment.

5. At the tenth representation, my dramatic career

was brought to a close by an unfortunate circumstance. We were playing the drama of "William Tell, the Hero of Switzerland." Of course I was William Tell, in spite of Fred Langdon, who wanted to act that character himself. I wouldn't let him, so he withdrew from the company, taking the only bow and arrow we had.

6. I made a crossbow out of a piece of whalebone, and did very well without him. We had reached that exciting scene where Gesler, the Austrian tyrant, commands Tell to shoot the apple from his son's head. Pepper Whitcomb, who played all the juvenile and women parts, was my son.

7. To guard against mischance, a piece of pasteboard was fastened by a handkerchief over the upper portion of Whitcomb's face, while the arrow to be used was sewed up in a strip of flannel. I was a capital marksman, and the big apple, only two yards distant, turned its russet cheek fairly towards me.

8. I can see poor little Pepper now, as he stood without flinching, waiting for me to perform my great feat. I raised the crossbow amid the breathless silence of the crowded audience—consisting of seven boys and three girls, exclusive of Kitty Collins, who insisted on paying her way in with a clothespin. I raised the crossbow, I repeat. Twang! went the whipcord; but, alas! instead of hitting the apple, the arrow flew right into Pepper Whitcomb's mouth, which happened to be open at the time, and destroyed my aim.

9. I shall never be able to banish that awful moment from my memory. Pepper's roar, expressive of astonishment, indignation, and pain, is still ringing in my ears. I looked upon him as a corpse, and, glanc-

ing not far into the dreary future, pictured myself led forth to execution in the presence of the very same spectators then assembled.

10. Luckily, poor Pepper was not seriously hurt; but Grandfather Nutter, appearing in the midst of the confusion (attracted by the howls of young Tell), issued an injunction against all theatricals thereafter, and the place was closed; not, however, without a farewell speech from me, in which I said that this

would have been the proudest moment of my life if I hadn't hit Pepper Whitcomb in the mouth. Whereupon the audience (assisted, I am glad to state, by Pepper) cried, "Hear! hear!"

11. I then attributed the accident to Pepper himself, whose mouth, being open at the instant I fired, acted upon the arrow much after the fashion of a whirlpool, and drew in the fatal shaft. I was about to explain how a comparatively small maelstrom could suck in the largest ship, when the curtain fell of its own accord, amid the shouts of the audience.

12. This was my last appearance on any stage. It was some time, though, before I heard the end of the William Tell business. Malicious little boys who hadn't been allowed to buy tickets to my theater used to cry out after me in the street,-"Who killed Cock Robin?'"

DEFINITIONS.—l. Cŏn´clāve, *a private meeting.* 2. Măn-a-ğē´ri-al, *of or pertaining to a manager.* 4. De-dŭct´ing, *taking away, subtracting.* 5. Ca-reer´, *course of action.* 8. Au´di-ençe, *an assembly of hearers.* 9. Ex-e-cū´tion, *a putting to death by law.* 10. In-jŭnc´tion, *a command.* 11. At-trĭb´ūt-ed, *assigned, charged.* Māel´strom (*pro.* māl´strum), *a whirlpool.*

Note.—The Revised Fifth Reader of this Series contains the portion of "William Tell" probably alluded to. See McGuffey's Fifth Reader, pp. 207-216.

LXXVII. ALFRED THE GREAT.

1. More than a thousand years ago, (in the year 849), a prince was born in England, who afterwards became one of the most celebrated and best loved kings in the world. His name was Alfred—afterwards called Alfred the Great—and he was the favorite son both of the king and queen.

2. In those days the common people were very ignorant; few of them could even read and write. There were no schools, and the monasteries, where almost the only teaching had been done, were nearly all destroyed in the wars which were continually going on. Only the higher classes had any chance to study, and even they paid much more attention to fighting than to studying.

3. But Alfred was different from most persons of his time. Even when a little boy, he delighted in listening to poems and to the ballads which harpers used to sing, and he learned many of them by heart. When he was twelve years old, his mother, the queen, offered to give a volume of poems to that one of her four sons who would first learn to read it. Alfred was the youngest of them all, yet he easily won the prize of which his brothers thought so little.

4. But, as has been said, these were stirring times, and Alfred was soon called on to show his great abilities as a soldier. The Danes, a warlike people, were continually swooping down in their vessels upon the coast of England. Often they spread over the entire country, plundering and burning the towns, and killing the people.

5. In the midst of these invasions Alfred became king, when he was only twenty-two years old. He proved as good a warrior as he was a student. He thought that whatever is worth doing at all is worth doing well. He was generally successful against the Danes, but at one time they seemed to have the country entirely in their power, and Alfred was compelled to hide for his life.

6. For some time he dressed as a peasant, and lived in the cottage of a cowherd, who was so careful of his king's safety that he did not even tell his wife who he was. So she treated the king as a common peasant, and one day gave him a sharp scolding because he allowed some cakes to burn on the griddle, after she had left him to watch them. She told him he was clever enough at eating cakes though he managed so badly at baking them.

7. When the search for him grew less active,

Alfred gradually collected some of his followers, with whom he encamped on a small spot of firm ground in the center of a bog. It was surrounded by almost impassable forests, and Alfred fortified the place so that it could not well be taken. Then he made frequent sudden and successful attacks on the enemy until his troops and the people became encouraged.

8. One victory in particular, when they captured a banner which the Danes thought enchanted, led Alfred to take bolder steps. He wished to find out the exact condition of the enemy, and, for this purpose, disguised himself as a harper and entered their camp. He was so successful in his disguise that he remained there some days, even being admitted to the tent of the Danish leader Guthrum.

9. He found their entire army living in careless security, and so he determined to make a sudden and bold attack on them, to try and rid his country once more of these cruel invaders. He summoned his people about him from far and wide. Many of them had long thought their beloved king dead, but now all eagerly obeyed his call.

10. He at once led them against that part of the camp which he had seen to be most unguarded. The attack was entirely unexpected; and, although the Danes were greater in numbers, they were defeated with great slaughter. Some of them, with their leader, fled to a fortified place, but were soon obliged to surrender.

11. Alfred granted them their lives, and settled them in a part of his kingdom where nearly all his own people had been destroyed. He hoped by this to change obstinate enemies into useful friends who would protect England from further attacks of their own

countrymen. However, some years later, when the Danes made another invasion, these people joined them in fighting against Alfred, but he soon succeeded in driving them all out of the country.

12. Much as Alfred did for his people in war, he did more in time of peace. Above all else he gave careful attention to their education. He rebuilt the monasteries and aided the young University of Oxford. He also founded many schools, to which every owner of a certain portion of land was compelled to send his children.

13. But he did as much good by the example that he set as by these acts. His time was divided into three parts. One was given to business, one to refreshment by sleep and food, and the third to study and devotion. Clocks and watches, and probably even sundials, were then unknown, so these divisions were marked by burning candles of equal lengths.

14. Alfred did not study for his own pleasure merely, but translated and wrote many works for the good of his people, using the simple language which they could easily understand and enjoy. His person was handsome and dignified, full of grace and activity. But the more noble beauty was within, in the enlightened mind and virtuous heart of the king. After his name, which has its place on an ancient record of English kings, is written the noble title of "Truth Teller."

DEFINITIONS.—2. Mŏn′as-tĕr-y, *a religious house where monks live.* 5. In-vā′ṣion, *the warlike entrance of an army.* 8. Dis-ḡuīṣed′, *hidden by an unusual dress and appearance.* 12. U-ni-vẽr′si-ty, *a school of the highest grade, in which are taught all branches of learning.* 14. Trans-lāt′ed, *changed from one language to another.* En-līght′ened, *well informed.*

LXXVII. LIVING ON A FARM.

1. How brightly through the mist of years,
   My quiet country home appears!
   My father busy all the day
   In plowing corn or raking hay;
   My mother moving with delight
   Among the milk pans, silver-bright;
   We children, just from school set free,
   Filling the garden with our glee.
   The blood of life was flowing warm
   When I was living on a farm.

2. I hear the sweet churchgoing bell,
   As o'er the fields its music fell,
   I see the country neighbors round
   Gathering beneath the pleasant sound;
   They stop awhile beside the door,
   To talk their homely matters o'er
   The springing corn, the ripening grain,
   And "how we need a little rain;"
   "A little sun would do no harm,
   We want good weather for the farm."

3. When autumn came, what joy to see
   The gathering of the husking bee,
   To hear the voices keeping tune,
   Of girls and boys beneath the moon,
   To mark the golden corn ears bright,
   More golden in the yellow light!
   Since I have learned the ways of men,
   I often turn to these again,
   And feel life wore its highest charm.
   When I was living on the farm.

LXXIX. HUGH IDLE AND MR. TOIL.

Adapted from the story of "Little Daffydowndilly," by **Nathaniel Hawthorne.** The author was born at Salem, Mass., in 1804, and ranks among the first of American novelists. He died in 1864.

1. Hugh Idle loved to do only what was agreeable, and took no delight in labor of any kind. But while Hugh was yet a little boy, he was sent away from home, and put under the care of a very strict schoolmaster, who went by the name of Mr. Toil.

2. Those who knew him best, affirmed that Mr. Toil was a very worthy character, and that he had done more good, both to children and grown people, than anybody else in the world. He had, however, a severe and ugly countenance; his voice was harsh; and all his ways and customs were disagreeable to our young friend, Hugh Idle.

3. The whole day long this terrible old schoolmaster sulked about among his scholars, with a big cane in his hand; and unless a lad chose to attend constantly and quietly to his book, he had no chance of enjoying a single quiet moment. "This will never do for me," thought Hugh; "I'll run off, and try to find my way home."

4. So the very next morning off he started, with only some bread and cheese for his breakfast, and very little pocket money to pay his expenses. He had gone but a short distance, when he overtook a man of grave and sedate appearance trudging at a moderate pace along the road.

5. "Good morning, my fine lad!" said the stranger; and his voice seemed hard and severe, yet had a sort of kindness in it; "whence do you come so early, and whither are you going?"

6. Now Hugh was a boy of very frank disposition, and had never been known to tell a lie in all his life. Nor did he tell one now, but confessed that he had run away from school on account of his great dislike to Mr. Toil. "Oh, very well, my little friend!" answered the stranger; "then we will go together; for I likewise have had a good deal to do with Mr. Toil, and should be glad to find some place where he was never heard of." So they walked on very sociably side by side.

7. By and by their road led them past a field, where some haymakers were at work. Hugh could not help thinking how much pleasanter it must be to make hay in the sunshine, under the blue sky, than to learn lessons all day long, shut up in a dismal school-room, continually watched by Mr. Toil.

8. But in the midst of these thoughts, while he was stopping to peep over the stone wall, he started back and caught hold of his companion's hand. "Quick, quick!" cried he; "let us run away, or he will catch us!"

9. "Who will catch us?" asked the stranger.

10. "Mr. Toil, the old schoolmaster," answered Hugh; "don't you see him among the haymakers?" and Hugh pointed to an elderly man, who seemed to be the owner of the field.

11. He was busily at work in his shirt sleeves. The drops of sweat stood upon his brow; and he kept constantly crying out to his work people to make hay while the sun shone. Strange to say, the features of the old farmer were precisely the same as those of Mr. Toil, who at that very moment must have been just entering the schoolroom.

12. "Don't be afraid," said the stranger; "this is not Mr. Toil, the schoolmaster, but a brother of his,

who was bred a farmer. He won't trouble you, unless you become a laborer on his farm."

13. Hugh believed what his companion said, but was glad when they were out of sight of the old farmer who bore such a singular resemblance to Mr. Toil. The two travelers came to a spot where some carpenters were building a house. Hugh begged his companion to stop awhile, for it was a pretty sight to see how neatly the carpenters did their work with their saws, planes, and hammers; and he was beginning to think he too should like to use the saw, and the plane, and the hammer, and be a carpenter himself. But suddenly he caught sight of something that made him seize his friend's hand, in a great fright.

14. "Make haste! quick, quick!" cried he; "there's old Mr. Toil again." The stranger cast his eyes where Hugh pointed his finger, and saw an elderly man, who seemed to be overseeing the carpenters, as he went to and fro about the unfinished house, marking out the work to be done, and urging the men to be diligent; and wherever he turned his hard and wrinkled visage, they sawed and hammered as if for dear life.

15. "Oh, no! this is not Mr. Toil, the schoolmaster," said the stranger; "it is another brother of his who follows the trade of carpenter."

16. "I am very glad to hear it," quoth Hugh; "but if you please, sir, I should like to get out of his way as soon as possible."

DEFINITIONS.—1. A-ḡree'a-ble, *pleasing.* 2. Af-fîrmed', *declared.* 4. Ex-pĕns'eş, *costs.* Se-dāte', *calm.* Mŏd'er-ate, *neither fast nor slow.* Dĭs-po-şĭ'tion, *natural state of mind.* Con-fĕssed', *ac-knowledged.* Sō'cia-bly, *in a friendly way.* 11. Fēat'ūreş, *the distinctive marks of the face.* 13. Re-şĕm'blançe, *likeness.* 14. Dĭl'i-ġent, *industrious.* Vĭş'aġe, *the face.* 16. Quōth, *said.*

LXXX. HUGH IDLE AND MR. TOIL.

(Concluded.)

1. Now Hugh and the stranger had not gone much further, when they met a company of soldiers, gayly dressed, with feathers in their caps, and glittering muskets on their shoulders. In front marched the drummers and fifers, making such merry music that Hugh would gladly have followed them to the end of the world. If he were only a soldier, he said to himself, old Mr. Toil would never venture to look him in the face.

2. "Quickstep! forward! march!" shouted a gruff voice.

3. Little Hugh started in great dismay; for this voice sounded precisely like that which he had heard every day in Mr. Toil's schoolroom. And turning his eyes to the captain of the company, what should he see but the very image of old Mr. Toil himself, in an officer's dress, to be sure, but looking as ugly and disagreeable as ever.

4. "This is certainly old Mr. Toil," said Hugh, in a trembling voice. "Let us away, for fear he should make us enlist in his company."

5. "You are mistaken again, my little friend," replied the stranger very composedly. "This is only a brother of Mr. Toil's, who has served in the army all his life. You and I need not be afraid of him."

6. "Well, well," said Hugh, "if you please, sir, I don't want to see the soldiers any more." So the child and the stranger resumed their journey; and, after awhile, they came to a house by the roadside, where a number of young men and rosy-cheeked girls,

with smiles on their faces, were dancing to the sound of a fiddle.

7. "Oh, let us stop here," cried Hugh; "Mr. Toil will never dare to show his face where there is a fiddler, and where people are dancing and making merry."

8. But the words had scarcely died away on the little boy's tongue, when, happening to cast his eyes on the fiddler, whom should he behold again but the likeness of Mr. Toil, armed with a fiddle bow this time, and flourishing it with as much ease and dexterity as if he had been a fiddler all his life.

9. "Oh, dear me!" whispered he, turning pale; "it seems as if there were nobody but Mr. Toil in the world."

10. "This is not your old schoolmaster," observed the stranger, "but another brother of his, who has learned to be a fiddler. He is ashamed of his family, and generally calls himself Master Pleasure; but his real name is Toil, and those who know him best think him still more disagreeable than his brothers."

11. "Pray, let us go on," said Hugh.

12. Well, thus the two went wandering along the highway and in shady lanes and through pleasant villages, and wherever they went, behold! there was the image of old Mr. Toil. If they entered a house, he sat in the parlor; if they peeped into the kitchen, he was there! He made himself at home in every cottage, and stole, under one disguise or another, into the most splendid mansions. Everywhere they stumbled on some of the old schoolmaster's innumerable brothers.

13. At length, little Hugh found himself completely worn out with running away from Mr. Toil. "Take

me back! take me back!" cried the poor fellow, bursting into tears. "If there is nothing but Toil all the world over, I may just as well go back to the school-house."

14. "Yonder it is; there is the schoolhouse!" said the stranger; for though he and little Hugh had taken a great many steps, they had traveled in a circle instead of a straight line. "Come, we will go back to the school together."

15. There was something in his companion's voice that little Hugh now remembered; and it is strange that he had not remembered it sooner. Looking up into his face, behold! there again was the likeness of old Mr. Toil, so that the poor child had been in company with Toil all day, even while he had been doing his best to run away from him.

16. Little Hugh Idle, however, had learned a good lesson, and from that time forward was diligent at his task, because he now knew that diligence is not a whit more toilsome than sport or idleness. And when he became better acquainted with Mr. Toil, he began to think his ways were not so disagreeable, and that the old schoolmaster's smile of approbation made his face sometimes appear almost as pleasant as even that of Hugh's mother.

DEFINITIONS.—1. Věn′tūre, *to dare, to risk.* 3. Dis-māy′, *fright, terror.* Pre-çīse′ly, *exactly.* 4. En-list′, *to put one's name on a roll, to join.* 5. Com-pōṣ′ed-ly, *calmly, quietly.* 6. Re-ṣūmed′, *recommenced.* 10. Ob-ṣerved′, *remarked.* 12. Ĭn-nū′mer-a-ble, *not to be counted.* 16. Ap-pro-bā′tion, *the act of regarding with pleasure.*

Exercises.—To whose school was Hugh Idle sent? Why did he run away? Relate the adventures of Hugh and the stranger. What lesson is taught by this story?

LXXXI. BURNING THE FALLOW.

Adapted from "Roughing it in the Bush," a story by **Mrs. Susanna Moodie** (sister of Agnes Strickland), who was born in Suffolk, England, in 1803. She died in 1885.

1. The day was sultry, and towards noon a strong wind sprang up that roared in the pine tops like the dashing of distant billows, but without in the least degree abating the heat. The children were lying listlessly upon the floor, and the girl and I were finishing sunbonnets, when Mary suddenly exclaimed, "Bless us, mistress, what a smoke!"

2. I ran immediately to the door, but was not able to distinguish ten yards before me. The swamp immediately below us was on fire, and the heavy wind was driving a dense black cloud of smoke directly towards us.

3. "What can this mean?" I cried. "Who can have set fire to the fallow?" As I ceased speaking, John Thomas stood pale and trembling before me. "John, what is the meaning of this fire?"

4. "Oh, ma'am, I hope you will forgive me; it was I set fire to it, and I would give all I have in the world if I had not done it."

5. "What is the danger?"

6. "Oh, I'm afraid that we shall all be burnt up," said John, beginning to whimper. "What shall we do?"

7. "Why, we must get out of it as fast as we can, and leave the house to its fate."

8. "We can't get out," said the man, in a low, hollow tone, which seemed the concentration of fear; "I

would have got out of it if I could; but just step to the back door, ma'am, and see."

9. Behind, before, on every side, we were surrounded by a wall of fire, burning furiously within a hundred yards of us, and cutting off all possibility of retreat; for, could we have found an opening through the burning heaps, we could not have seen our way through the dense canopy of smoke; and, buried as we were in the heart of the forest, no one could discover our situation till we were beyond the reach of help.

10. I closed the door, and went back to the parlor. Fear was knocking loudly at my heart, for our utter helplessness destroyed all hope of our being able to effect our escape. The girl sat upon the floor by the children, who, unconscious of the peril that hung over them, had both fallen asleep. She was silently weeping; while the boy who had caused the mischief was crying aloud.

11. A strange calm succeeded my first alarm. I sat down upon the step of the door, and watched the awful scene in silence. The fire was raging in the cedar swamp immediately below the ridge on which the house stood, and it presented a spectacle truly appalling.

12. From out of the dense folds of a canopy of black smoke—the blackest I ever saw—leaped up red forks of lurid flame as high as the tree tops, igniting the branches of a group of tall pines that had been left for saw logs. A deep gloom blotted out the heavens from our sight. The air was filled with fiery particles, which floated even to the doorstep—while the crackling and roaring of the flames might have been heard at a great distance.

13. To reach the shore of the lake, we must pass through the burning swamp, and not a bird could pass over it with unscorched wings. The fierce wind drove the flames at the sides and back of the house up the clearing; and our passage to the road or to the forest, on the right and left, was entirely obstructed by a sea of flames. Our only ark of safety was the house, so long as it remained untouched by the fire.

14. I turned to young Thomas, and asked him how long he thought that would he. "When the fire clears this little ridge in front, ma'am. The Lord have mercy on us then, or we must all go."

15. I threw myself down on the floor beside my children, and pressed them to my heart, while inwardly I thanked God that they were asleep, unconscious of danger, and unable by their cries to distract our attention from adopting any plan which might offer to effect their escape.

16. The heat soon became suffocating. We were parched with thirst, and there was not a drop of water in the house, and none to be procured nearer than the lake. I turned once more to the door, hoping that a passage might have been burnt through to the water. I saw nothing but a dense cloud of fire and smoke— could hear nothing but the crackling and roaring of flames, which was gaining so fast upon us that I felt their scorching breath in my face.

17. "Ah," thought I—and it was a most bitter thought—"what will my beloved husband say when he returns and finds that his poor wife and his dear girls have perished in this miserable manner? But God can save us yet."

18. The thought had scarcely found a voice in my heart before the wind rose to a hurricane, scattering

the flames on all sides into a tempest of burning billows. I buried my head in my apron, for I thought that all was lost, when a most terrific crash of thunder burst over our heads, and, like the breaking of a waterspout, down came the rushing torrent of rain which had been pent up for so many weeks.

19. In a few minutes the chip yard was all afloat, and the fire effectually checked. The storm which, unnoticed by us, had been gathering all day, and which was the only one of any note we had that summer, continued to rage all night, and before morning had quite subdued the cruel enemy whose approach we had viewed with such dread.

Definitions.-l. A-bāt'ing, *lessening.* Lĭst'less-ly, *not paying attention, heedlessly.* 3. Făl'lōw, *a new clearing usually covered with brush heaps.* 8. Cŏn-çen-trā'tion, *bringing into a small space, the essence.* 9. Căn'o-py, *a covering or curtain.* 10. Ef-fĕct', *to bring to pass.* 11. Suc-çeed'ed, *followed.* Ap-pạll'ing, *terrifying.* 12. Lū'rid, *dull red.* Ĭg-nīt'ing, *setting on fire.* 15. Dis-trăct', *confuse, perplex.* 16. Pärched, *made very dry.* 18. Wạ'ter-spout, *a column of water caught up by a whirlwind.*

LXXXII. THE DYING SOLDIERS.

1. A waste of land, a sodden plain,
    A lurid sunset sky,
  With clouds that fled and faded fast
    In ghostly phantasy;
  A field upturned by trampling feet,
    A field uppiled with slain,
  With horse and rider blent in death
    Upon the battle plain.

2. The dying and the dead lie low;
　　For them, no more shall rise
　The evening moon, nor midnight stars,
　　Nor day light's soft surprise:
　They will not wake to tenderest call,
　　Nor see again each home,
　Where waiting hearts shall throb and break,
　　When this day's tidings come.

3. Two soldiers, lying as they fell
　　Upon the reddened clay—
　In daytime, foes; at night, in peace
　　Breathing their lives away!
　Brave hearts had stirred each manly breast;
　　Fate only, made them foes;
　And lying, dying, side by side,
　　A softened feeling rose.

4. "Our time is short," one faint voice said;
　　"To-day we've done our best
　On different sides: what matters now?
　　To-morrow we shall rest!
　Life lies behind. I might not care
　　For only my own sake;
　But far away are other hearts,
　　That this day's work will break.

5. "Among New Hampshire's snowy hills,
　　There pray for me to-night
　A woman, and a little girl
　　With hair like golden light;"
　And at the thought, broke forth, at last,
　　The cry of anguish wild,
　That would not longer be repressed
　　"O God, my wife, my child!"

6. "And," said the other dying man,
   "Across the Georgia plain,
There watch and wait for me loved ones
   I ne'er shall see again:
A little girl, with dark, bright eyes,
   Each day waits at the door;
Her father's step, her father's kiss,
   Will never greet her more.

7. "To-day we sought each other's lives:
   Death levels all that now;
For soon before God's mercy seat
   Together we shall bow.
Forgive each other while we may;
   Life's but a weary game,
And, right or wrong, the morning sun
   Will find us, dead, the same."

8. The dying lips the pardon breathe;
   The dying hands entwine;
The last ray fades, and over all
   The stars from heaven shine;
And the little girl with golden hair,
   And one with dark eyes bright,
On Hampshire's hills, and Georgia's plain,
   Were fatherless that night!

DEFINITIONS.—1. Sŏd'den, *soaked.* Phăn'ta-sy, *specter-like appearance.* Blĕnt, *mingled together.* 2. Tī'dings, *news.* 5. An'-ġuish, *deep distress.* Re-prĕssed', *kept back.* 8. Pär'don, *forgiveness.* En-twīne', *clasp together.*

EXERCISE.—What do the first two stanzas describe? What does the third? What did one soldier say to the other? Where was his home? What friends had he there? Where was the home of the other soldier? Who waited for him? Did they forgive each other?

LXXXIII. THE ATTACK ON NYMWEGEN.

From "The History of the United Netherlands," by **John Lothrop Motley**, who was born in 1814, at Dorchester, Mass. He graduated at Harvard in 1831, and afterwards lived many years In Europe, writing the histories which made him famous. He died in 1877.

1. On the evening of the 10th of August, 1589, there was a wedding feast in one of the splendid mansions of the stately city. The festivities were prolonged until deep in the midsummer's night, and harp and viol were still inspiring the feet of the dancers, when on a sudden, in the midst of the holiday groups, appeared the grim visage of Martin Schenk, the man who never smiled.

2. Clad in no wedding garment, but in armor of proof, with morion on head, and sword in hand, the great freebooter strode heavily through the ball-room, followed by a party of those terrible musketeers who never gave or asked for quarter, while the affrighted revelers fluttered away before them.

3. Taking advantage of a dark night, he had just dropped down the river from his castle, with five and twenty barges, had landed with his most trusted soldiers in the foremost vessels, had battered down the gate of St. Anthony, and surprised and slain the guard.

4. Without waiting for the rest of his boats, he had then stolen with his comrades through the silent streets, and torn away the latticework, and other slight defenses on the rear of the house which they had now entered, and through which they intended to possess themselves of the market place.

5. Martin had long since selected this mansion as a proper position for his enterprise, but he had not been bidden to the wedding, and was somewhat disconcerted

when he found himself on the festive scene which he had so grimly interrupted.

6. Some of the merrymakers escaped from the house, and proceeded to alarm the town; while Schenk hastily fortified his position, and took possession of the square. But the burghers and garrison were soon on foot, and he was driven back into the house.

7. Three times he recovered the square by main strength of his own arm, seconded by the handful of

men whom he had brought with him, and three times he was beaten back by overwhelming numbers into the wedding mansion.

8. The arrival of the greater part of his followers, with whose assistance he could easily have mastered the city in the first moments of surprise, was mysteriously delayed. He could not account for their prolonged absence, and was meanwhile supported only by those who had arrived with him in the foremost barges.

9. The truth—of which he was ignorant—was, that the remainder of the flotilla, borne along by the strong and deep current of the Waal, then in a state of freshet, had shot past the landing place, and had ever since been vainly struggling against wind and tide to force their way back to the necessary point.

10. Meantime Schenk and his followers fought desperately in the market place, and desperately in the house which he had seized. But a whole garrison, and a town full of citizens in arms proved too much for him, and he was now hotly besieged in the mansion, and at last driven forth into the streets.

11. By this time day was dawning, the whole population, soldiers and burghers, men, women, and children, were thronging about the little band of marauders, and assailing them with every weapon and every missile to be found. Schenk fought with his usual ferocity, but at last the musketeers, in spite of his indignant commands, began rapidly to retreat toward the quay.

12. In vain Martin stormed and cursed, in vain with his own hand he struck more than one of his soldiers dead. He was swept along with the panic-stricken band, and when, shouting and gnashing his

teeth with frenzy, he reached the quay at last, he saw at a glance why his great enterprise had failed.

13. The few empty barges of his own party were moored at the steps; the rest were half a mile off, contending hopelessly against the swollen and rapid Waal. Schenk, desperately wounded, was left almost alone upon the wharf, for his routed followers had plunged helter-skelter into the boats, several of which, overladen in the panic, sank at once, leaving the soldiers to drown or struggle with the waves.

14. The game was lost. Nothing was left the freebooter but retreat. Reluctantly turning his back on his enemies, now in full cry close behind him, Schenk sprang into the last remaining boat just pushing from the quay. Already overladen, it foundered with his additional weight, and Martin Schenk, encumbered with his heavy armor, sank at once to the bottom of the Waal.

15. Some of the fugitives succeeded in swimming down the stream, and were picked up by their comrades in the barges below the town, and so made their escape. Many were drowned with their captain. A few days afterward, the inhabitants of Nymwegen fished up the body of the famous partisan. He was easily recognized by his armor, and by his truculent face, still wearing the scowl with which he had last rebuked his followers.

DEFINITIONS.—2. Mō'ri-on, *a kind of helmet.* Free'bōōt-er, *one who plunders.* Mŭs-ket-eer', *a soldier armed with a musket.* Quar'ter, *mercy.* 6. Bûrgh'ers, *inhabitants of a town.* Găr'ri-son, *troops stationed in a fort or town.* 9. Flo-tǐl'lä, *a fleet of small vessels.* 11. Ma-raud'ers, *plunderers.* Quay (*pro.* kē), *a wharf.* 14. Foun'dered, *sank.* En-cŭm'bered, *weighed down.* 15. Pär'ti-san, *a commander of a body of roving troops.* Trŭ'cu-lent, *fierce.*

LXXXIV. THE SEASONS.

I. SPRING.

H. G. Adams, an English writer, has compiled two volumes of poetical quotations, and is the author of several volumes of original poems. The following is from the "Story of the Seasons."

A bursting into greenness;
　　A waking as from sleep;
A twitter and a warble
　　That make the pulses leap:
A watching, as in childhood,
　　For the flowers that, one by one,
Open their golden petals
　　To woo the fitful sun.
A gust, a flash, a gurgle,
　　A wish to shout and sing,
As, filled with hope and gladness,
　　We hail the vernal Spring.

II. SUMMER.

Now is the high tide of the year,
　　And whatever of life hath ebbed away
Comes flooding back with a ripply cheer,
　　Into every bare inlet and creek and bay.
We may shut our eyes, but we can not help knowing
That skies are clear and grass is growing;
The breeze comes whispering in our ear,
That dandelions are blossoming near,
　　That maize has sprouted, that streams are flowing,
That the river is bluer than the sky,
That the robin is plastering his house hard by;
And if the breeze kept the good news back
For other couriers we should not lack;

We could guess it all by yon heifer's lowing,—
And hark! how clear bold chanticleer,
Warmed with the new wine of the year,
    Tells all in his lusty crowing.

                                        —*Lowell.*

III. AUTUMN.

Thomas Hood, author of the following selection, was born in 1798, at London, where he was editor of the "London Magazine," and died in 1845. He is best known as a humorist, but some of his poems are full of tender feeling.

    The autumn is old;
    The sear leaves are flying;
    He hath gathered up gold
    And now he is dying:
    Old age, begin sighing!

    The year's in the wane;
    There is nothing adorning;
    The night has no eve,
    And the day has no morning;
    Cold winter gives warning.

IV. WINTER.

Charles T. Brooks translated the following selection from the original by the German poet, Ludwig Holty. Mr. Brooks was born at Salem, Mass., in 1813. After graduation at Harvard he entered the ministry. He translated much from the German, both of poetry and prose. He died in 1883.

    Now no plumed throng
    Charms the wood with song;
    Icebound trees are glittering;
    Merry snowbirds, twittering,
        Fondly strive to cheer
        Scenes so cold and drear.

Winter, still I see
Many charms in thee,
Love thy chilly greeting,
Snowstorms fiercely beating,
And the dear delights
Of the long, long nights.

DEFINITIONS.—(I.) Pĕt′alṣ, *the colored leaves of flowers.*
Vĕr′-nal, *belonging to spring.* (II.) Ebbed, *flowed back, receded.*
Cọu′rier (*pro.* kōō′rĭ-er), *a messenger.* Lŭs′ty, *strong, vigorous,*
health-ful. (III.) Sēar, *dry, withered.* Wāne, *decrease, decline.*

LXXXV. BRANDYWINE FORD.

Bayard Taylor was born at Kennett Square, Penn., in 1825. He received a limited school education, but at an early age displayed great energy and talent. He was a great traveler, and a fluent, graceful writer, both of prose and verse. Mr. Taylor held high official positions under the government. The following selection is adapted from "The Story of Kennett,"

1. The black, dreary night, seemed interminable. He could only guess, here and there, at a landmark, and was forced to rely more upon Roger's instinct of the road than upon the guidance of his senses. Toward midnight, as he judged, by the solitary crow of a cock, the rain almost entirely ceased.

2. The wind began to blow sharp and keen, and the hard vault of the sky to lift a little. He fancied that the hills on his right had fallen away, and that the horizon was suddenly depressed towards the north. Roger's feet began to splash in constantly deepening water, and presently a roar, distinct from that of the wind, filled the air.

3. It was the Brandywine. The stream had over-flowed its broad meadow bottoms, and was running high and fierce beyond its main channel. The turbid waters made a dim, dusky gleam around him; soon the fences disappeared, and the flood reached to his horse's body.

4. But he knew that the ford could be distinguished by the break in the fringe of timber; moreover, that the creek bank was a little higher than the meadows behind it, and so far, at least, he might venture. The ford was not more than twenty yards across, and he could trust Roger to swim that distance.

5. The faithful animal pressed bravely on, but Gilbert soon noticed that he seemed at fault. The swift water had forced him out of the road, and he stopped from time to time, as if anxious and uneasy. The timber could now be discerned, only a short distance in advance, and in a few minutes they would gain the bank.

6. What was that? A strange, rustling, hissing sound, as of cattle trampling through dry reeds,—a sound which quivered and shook, even in the breath of the hurrying wind! Roger snorted, stood still, and trembled in every limb; and a sensation of awe and terror struck a chill through Gilbert's heart. The sound drew swiftly nearer, and became a wild, seething roar, filling the whole breadth of the valley.

7. "The dam! the dam!" cried Gilbert, "the dam has given way!" He turned Roger's head, gave him the rein, struck, spurred, cheered, and shouted. The brave beast struggled through the impeding flood, but the advance wave of the coming inundation already touched his side. He staggered; a line of churning foam bore down upon them, the terrible roar was all

around and over them, and horse and rider were whirled away.

8. What happened during the first few seconds, Gilbert could never distinctly recall. Now they were whelmed in the water, now riding its careering tide, torn through the tops of brushwood, jostled by floating logs and timbers of the dam, but always, as it seemed, remorselessly held in the heart of the tumult and the ruin.

9. He saw at last that they had fallen behind the furious onset of the flood, but Roger was still swimming with it, desperately throwing up his head from time to time, and snorting the water from his nostrils. All his efforts to gain a foothold failed; his strength was nearly spent, and unless some help should come in a few minutes it would come in vain. And in the darkness, and the rapidity with which they were borne along, how should help come?

10. All at once Roger's course stopped. He became an obstacle to the flood, which pressed him against some other obstacle below, and rushed over horse and rider. Thrusting out his hand, Gilbert felt the rough bark of a tree. Leaning towards it, and clasping the log in his arms, he drew himself from the saddle, while Roger, freed from his burden, struggled into the current and instantly disappeared.

11. As nearly as Gilbert could ascertain, several timbers, thrown over each other, had lodged, probably upon a rocky islet in the stream, the uppermost one projecting slantingly out of the flood. It required all his strength to resist the current which sucked, and whirled, and tugged at his body, and to climb high enough to escape its force, without overbalancing his support. At last, though still half immerged, he

found himself comparatively safe for a time, yet as far as ever from a final rescue.

12. Yet a new danger now assailed him, from the increasing cold. There was already a sting of frost, a breath of ice, in the wind. In another hour the sky was nearly swept bare of clouds, and he could note the lapse of the night by the sinking of the moon. But he was by this time hardly in a condition to note anything more.

DEFINITIONS.—1. In-tẽr'mi-na-ble, *endless.* 2. De-prẽssed', *low-ered.* 3. Tûr'bid, *muddy.* 5. Diṣ-çẽrncd' (*pro.* diz-zẽrned'), *made out, distinguished.* 6. Seeth'ing, *boiling, bubbling.* 7. Im-pēd'ing, *hindering, obstucting.* In-un-dā'tion, *a flood.* 9. On'sĕt, *a rushing upon, attack.* 11. Im-mẽrġed', *plunged under a liquid.* 12. Lăpse, *a gradual passing away.*

LXXXVI. BRANDYWINE FORD.

(CONCLUDED.)

1. The moon was low in the west, and there was a pale glimmer of the coming dawn in the sky, when Gilbert Potter suddenly raised his head. Above the noise of the water and the whistle of the wind, he heard a familiar sound,—the shrill, sharp neigh of a horse. Lifting himself with great exertion, to a sitting posture, he saw two men, on horseback, in the flooded meadow, a little below him. They stopped, seemed to consult, and presently drew nearer.

2. Gilbert tried to shout, but the muscles of his throat were stiff, and his lungs refused to act. The horse neighed again. This time there was no mistake;

it was Roger that he heard! Voice came to him, and he cried aloud,—a hoarse, strange, unnatural cry.

The horsemen heard it, and rapidly pushed up the bank, until they reached a point directly opposite to him. The prospect of escape brought a thrill of life to his frame; he looked around and saw that the flood had indeed fallen.

3. "We have no rope," he heard one of the men say. "How shall we reach him?"

"There is no time to get one now," the other answered. "My horse is stronger than yours. I'll go into the creek just below, where it's broader and not so deep, and work my way up to him,"

"But one horse can't carry both."

"His will follow, be sure, when it sees me."

4. As the last speaker moved away, Gilbert saw a led horse plunging through the water beside the other. It was a difficult and dangerous undertaking. The horseman and the loose horse entered the main stream below, where its divided channel met and broadened, but it was still above the saddle girths, and very swift.

5. Sometimes the animals plunged, losing their foothold; nevertheless, they gallantly breasted the current, and inch by inch worked their way to a point about six feet below Gilbert. It seemed impossible to approach nearer.

"Can you swim?" asked the man.

Gilbert shook his head. "Throw me the end of Roger's bridle!" he then cried.

6. The man unbuckled the bridle and threw it, keeping the end of the rein in his hand. Gilbert tried to grasp it, but his hands were too numb. He managed, however, to get one arm and his head through the opening, and relaxed his hold on the log.

7. A plunge, and the man had him by the collar. He felt himself lifted by a strong arm and laid across Roger's saddle. With his failing strength and stiff limbs, it was no slight task to get into place; and the return, though less laborious to the horses, was equally dangerous, because Gilbert was scarcely able to support himself without help.

"You're safe now," said the man, when they reached the bank, "but it's a downright mercy of God that you're alive!"

8. The other horseman joined them, and they rode slowly across the flooded meadow. They had both thrown their cloaks around Gilbert, and carefully steadied him in the saddle, one on each side. He was too much exhausted to ask how they had found him, or whither they were taking him,—too numb for curiosity, almost for gratitude.

9. "Here's your savior!" said one of the men, patting Roger's shoulder. "It was through him that we found you. Do you wish to know how? Well— about three o'clock it was, maybe a little earlier, maybe a little later, my wife woke me up. 'Do you hear that?' she said.

10. "I listened and heard a horse in the lane before the door, neighing,—I can't tell you exactly how it was,—as though he would call up the house. It was rather queer, I thought, so I got up and looked out of the window, and it seemed to me he had a saddle on. He stamped, and pawed, and then he gave another neigh, and stamped again.

11. "Said I to my wife, 'There is something wrong here,' and I dressed and went out. When he saw me, he acted in the strangest way you ever saw; thought I, if ever an animal wanted to speak, that animal does.

When I tried to catch him, he shot off, ran down the lane a bit, and then came back acting as strangely as ever.

12. "I went into the house and woke up my brother, here, and we saddled our horses and started. Away went yours ahead, stopping every minute to look around and see if we followed. When we came to the water I rather hesitated, but it was of no use; the horse would have us go on and on, till we found you. I never heard of such a thing before, in all my life." Gilbert did not speak, but two large tears slowly gathered in his eyes, and rolled down his cheeks. The men saw his emotion, and respected it.

13. In the light of the cold, keen dawn, they reached a snug farmhouse, a mile from the Brandywine. The men lifted Gilbert from the saddle, and would have carried him immediately into the house, but he first leaned upon Roger's neck, took the faithful creature's head in his arms, and kissed it.

DEFINITIONS.—2. Prŏs'peet, *ground or reason for hoping, anticipation.* 5. Brĕast'ed (*pro.* brĕst'ed), *opposed courageously.* 6. Nŭmb, *without the power of feeling or motion.* Re-lăxed', *loosened.* 12. E-mō'tion, *excited feeling, agitation.*

LXXXVII. THE BEST CAPITAL

Louisa May Alcott was born at Germantown, Pa., in 1833, and, among other works, wrote many beautiful stories for children. During the Civil War she was a hospital nurse at Washington. The following selection is adapted from "Little Men." She died in 1888.

1. One would have said that modest John Brooke, in his busy, quiet, humble life, had had little time to make friends; but now they seemed to start up every-

where,—old and young, rich and poor, high and low; for all unconsciously his influence had made itself widely felt, his virtues were remembered, and his hidden charities rose up to bless him.

2. The group about his coffin was a far more eloquent eulogy than any that man could utter. There were the rich men whom he had served faithfully for years; the poor old women whom he cherished with his little store, in memory of his mother; the wife to whom he had given such happiness that death could not mar it utterly; the brothers and sisters in whose hearts he had made a place forever; the little son and daughter who already felt the loss of his strong arm and tender voice; the young children, sobbing for their kindest playmate, and the tall lads, watching with softened faces a scene which they never could forget.

3. That evening, as the Plumfield boys sat on the steps, as usual, in the mild September moonlight, they naturally fell to talking of the event of the day.

Emil began by breaking out in his impetuous way, "Uncle Fritz is the wisest, and Uncle Laurie the jolliest, but Uncle John was the best; and I'd rather be like him than any man I ever saw."

4. "So would I. Did you hear what those gentlemen said to Grandpa to-day? I would like to have that said of me when I was dead;" and Franz felt with regret that he had not appreciated Uncle John enough.

"What did they say?" asked Jack, who had been much impressed by the scenes of the day.

5. "Why, one of the partners of Mr. Laurence, where Uncle John has been ever so long, was saying that he was conscientious almost to a fault as a busi-

ness man, and above reproach in all things. Another gentleman said no money could repay the fidelity and honesty with which Uncle John had served him, and then Grandpa told them the best of all.

6. "Uncle John once had a place in the office of a man who cheated, and when this man wanted uncle to help him do it, uncle wouldn't, though he was offered a big salary. The man was angry, and said, 'You will never get on in business with such strict principles;' and uncle answered back, 'I never will try to get on without them,' and left the place for a much harder and poorer one."

7. "Good !" cried several of the boys warmly, for they were in the mood to understand and value the little story as never before.

"He wasn't rich, was he?" asked Jack.

"No."

"He never did anything to make a stir in the world, did he?"

"No."

"He was only good?"

"That's all;" and Franz found himself wishing that Uncle John had done something to boast of, for it was evident that Jack was disappointed by his replies.

8. "Only good. That is all and everything," said Uncle Fritz, who had overheard the last few words, and guessed what was going on in the minds of the lads.

"Let me tell you a little about John Brooke, and you will see why men honor him, and why he was satisfied to be good rather than rich or famous. He simply did his duty in all things, and did it so cheerfully, so faithfully, that it kept him patient, brave, and happy, through poverty and loneliness and years of hard work.

9. "He was a good son, and gave up his own plans to stay and live with his mother while she needed him. He was a good friend, and taught your Uncle Laurie much beside his Greek and Latin, did it unconsciously, perhaps, by showing him an example of an upright man.

10. "He was a faithful servant, and made himself so valuable to those who employed him that they will find it hard to fill his place. He was a good husband and father, so tender, wise, and thoughtful, that Laurie and I learned much of him, and only knew how well he loved his family when we discovered all he had done for them, unsuspected and unassisted."

11. Uncle Fritz stopped a minute, and the boys sat like statues in the moonlight until he went on again, in a subdued and earnest voice: "As he lay dying, I said to him, 'Have no care for your wife and the little ones; I will see that they never want.' Then he smiled and pressed my hand, and answered, in his cheerful way, 'No need of that; I have cared for them.'

12. "And so he had, for when we looked among his papers, all was in order,—not a debt remained; and safely put away was enough to keep his wife comfortable and independent. Then we knew why he had lived so plainly, denied himself so many pleasures, except that of charity, and worked so hard that I fear he shortened his good life.

13. "He never asked help for himself, though often for others, but bore his own burden and worked out his own task bravely and quietly. No one can say a word of complaint against him, so just and generous

and kind was he; and now, when he is gone, all find so much to love and praise and honor, that I am proud to have been his friend, and would rather leave my children the legacy he leaves his than the largest fortune ever made.

14. "Yes! simple, genuine goodness is the best capital to found the business of this life upon. It lasts when fame and money fail, and is the only riches we can take out of this world with us. Remember that, my boys; and, if you want to earn respect and confidence and love, follow in the footsteps of John Brooke."

DEFINITIONS.—2. Eū′lo-ġy, *a speech or writing in praise of the character of a person.* Chĕr′ished, *supported, nurtured with care.* 4. Ap-prē′ci-āt-ed (*pro.* ap-prē′shĭ-āt-ed), *valued justly.* 5. Cŏn-sci-ĕn′tioŭs (*pro.* kŏn-shĭ-ĕn′shŭs), *governed by a strict regard to the rules of right and wrong.* 7. Mōōd, *state of mind, disposition.* 11. Sub-dūed′, *reduced to tenderness, softened.* 12. In-de-pĕnd′ent, *not relying on others.* 13. Lĕġ′a-çy, *a gift by will, a bequest.* 14. Căp′i-tal *stock employed in any business.*

LXXXVIII. THE INCHCAPE ROCK.

Robert Southey was a celebrated English poet, born 1774, who once held the honorable position of poet laureate. He wrote a great deal both in prose and verse.

1. No stir in the air, no stir in the sea,
   The ship was as still as she could be,
   Her sails from heaven received no motion,
   Her keel was steady in the ocean.

2. Without either sign or sound of their shock
   The waves flowed over the Inchcape Rock;
   So little they rose, so little they fell,
   They did not move the Inchcape Bell.

3. The good old Abbot of Aberbrothok
   Had placed that bell on the Inchcape Rock;
   On a buoy in the storm it floated and swung,
   And over the waves its warning rung.

4. When the Rock was hid by the surges' swell,
   The mariners heard the warning bell;
   And then they knew the perilous Rock,
   And blest the Abbot of Aberbrothok.

5. The sun in heaven was shining gay,
   All things were joyful on that day;
   The sea birds screamed as they wheeled round,
   And there was joyance in their sound.

6. The buoy of the Inchcape Bell was seen
   A darker speck on the ocean green;
   Sir Ralph the Rover walked his deck,
   And he fixed his eye on the darker speck.

7. He felt the cheering power of spring,
   It made him whistle, it made him sing;
   His heart was mirthful to excess,
   But the Rover's mirth was wickedness.

8. His eye was on the Inchcape float;
   Quoth he, "My men put out the boat,
   And row me to the Inchcape Rock,
   And I'll plague the Abbot of Aberbrothok."

9. The boat is lowered, the boatmen row,
   And to the Inchcape Rock they go;
   Sir Ralph bent over from the boat,
   And he cut the bell from the Inchcape float.

10. Down sunk the bell, with a gurgling sound,
    The bubbles rose and burst around;
    Quoth Sir Ralph, "The next who comes to the
        Rock,
    Won't bless the Abbot of Aberbrothok."

11. Sir Ralph the Rover sailed away,
    He scoured the seas for many a day;
    And now grown rich with plundered store,
    He steers his course for Scotland's shore.

12. So thick a haze o'erspreads the sky
    They can not see the sun on high;
    The wind hath blown a gale all day,
    At evening it hath died away.

13. On the deck the Rover takes his stand,
    So dark it is they see no land.
    Quoth Sir Ralph, "It will be lighter soon,
    For there is the dawn of the rising moon."

14. "Canst hear," said one, "the breakers roar?
    For methinks we should be near the shore."
    "Now where we are I can not tell,
    But I wish I could hear the Inchcape Bell."

15. They hear no sound, the swell is strong;
    Though the wind hath fallen, they drift along,
    Till the vessel strikes with a shivering shock:
    Cried they, "It is the Inchcape Rock!"

16. Sir Ralph the rover tore his hair,
    He curst himself in his despair;
    The waves rush in on every side,
    The ship is sinking beneath the tide.

17. But even in his dying fear
    One dreadful sound could the Rover hear,
    A sound as if with the Inchcape Bell
    The fiends below were ringing his knell.

DEFINITIONS.—1. Keel, *the principal timber in a ship, extending from bow to stern, at the bottom.* 3. Buoy, (*pro.* bwọy *or* bwôў) *a float-ing mark to point out the position of rocks, etc., beneath the water.* 4. Sûrġe, *a large wave.* 6. Joy'ançe, *gayety.* 11. Scoured, *roved over, ranged about.* Stōre, *that which is massed together.* 14. Me-thĭnks', *it seems to me.* 17. Fiēnds (*pro.* fĕndṣ), *evil spirits.* Knĕll (*pro.* nĕl), *the stroke of a bell rung at a funeral or at the death of a person.*

NOTES.—The above poem was written at Bristol, England, in 1802, and recounts an old tradition.

2. The Inchcape Rock is at the entrance of the Frith of Tay, Scotland, about fifteen miles from shore.

LXXXIX. MY MOTHER'S GRAVE.

1. It was thirteen years since my mother's death, when, after a long absence from my native village, I stood beside the sacred mound beneath which I had seen her buried. Since that mournful period, a great change had come over me. My childish years had passed away, and with them my youthful character. The world was altered, too; and as I stood at my mother's grave, I could hardly realize that I was the same thoughtless, happy creature, whose checks she so often kissed in an excess of tenderness.

2. But the varied events of thirteen years had not effaced the remembrance of that mother's smile. It seemed as if I had seen her but yesterday—as if the blessed sound of her well-remembered voice was in my ear. The gay dreams of my infancy and childhood were brought back so distinctly to my mind that, had it not been for one bitter recollection, the tears I shed would have been gentle and refreshing.

3. The circumstance may seem a trifling one, but the thought of it now pains my heart; and I relate it, that those children who have parents to love them may learn to value them as they ought. My mother had been ill a long time, and I had become so accus-

stomed to her pale face and weak voice, that I was not frightened at them, as children usually are. At first, it is true, I sobbed violently; but when, day after day, I returned from school, and found her the same, I began to believe she would always be spared to me; but they told me she would die.

4. One day when I had lost my place in the class, I came home discouraged and fretful. I went to my mother's chamber. She was paler than usual, but she met me with the same affectionate smile that always welcomed my return. Alas! when I look back through the lapse of thirteen years, I think my heart must have been stone not to have been melted by it. She requested me to go downstairs and bring her a glass of water. I pettishly asked her why she did not call a domestic to do it. With a look of mild re-proach, which I shall never forget if I live to be a hundred years old, she said, "Will not my daughter bring a glass of water for her poor, sick mother?"

5. I went and brought her the water, but I did not do it kindly. Instead of smiling, and kissing her as I had been wont to do, I set the glass down very quickly, and left the room. After playing a short time, I went to bed without bidding my mother good night; but when alone in my room, in darkness and silence, I remembered how pale she looked, and how her voice trembled when she said, "Will not my daughter bring a glass of water for her poor, sick mother?" I could not sleep. I stole into her cham-ber to ask forgiveness. She had sunk into an easy slumber, and they told me I must not waken her.

6. I did not tell anyone what troubled me, but stole back to my bed, resolved to rise early in the morning and tell her how sorry I was for my con-

duct. The sun was shining brightly when I awoke, and, hurrying on my clothes, I hastened to my mother's chamber. She was dead! She never spoke more—never smiled upon me again; and when I touched the hand that used to rest upon my head in blessing, it was so cold that it made me start.

7. I bowed down by her side, and sobbed in the bitterness of my heart. I then wished that I might die, and be buried with her; and, old as I now am, I would give worlds, were they mine to give, could my mother but have lived to tell me she forgave my childish ingratitude. But I can not call her back; and when I stand by her grave, and whenever I think of her manifold kindness, the memory of that reproachful look she gave me will bite like a serpent and sting like an adder.

DEFINITION's.—1. Mōurn'fụl, *full of sorrow.* Rḗal-īze, *to cause to seem real.* Ex-çĕss', *that which goes beyond what is usual.* 2. Vā'ried, *different.* Ef-fāced', *worn away.* Pĕt'tish-ly, *in an ill-tempered way.* 6. Re-şŏlved, *determined.* 7. In-ḡrăt'i-tūde, *unthankfulness.* Măn'i-fōld. *various, multiplied.*

XC. A MOTHER'S GIFT-THE BIBLE.

1. Remember, love, who gave thee this,
    When other days shall come,
When she who had thine earliest kiss,
    Sleeps in her narrow home.
Remember! 'twas a mother gave
The gift to one she'd die to save!

2. That mother sought a pledge of love,
  The holiest for her son,
And from the gifts of God above,
  She chose a goodly one;
She chose for her beloved boy,
The source of light, and life, and joy.

3. She bade him keep the gift, that, when
  The parting hour should come,
They might have hope to meet again
  In an eternal home.
She said his faith in this would be
Sweet incense to her memory.

4. And should the scoffer, in his pride,
  Laugh that fond faith to scorn,
And bid him cast the pledge aside,
  That he from youth had borne,
She bade him pause, and ask his breast
If SHE or HE had loved him best.

5. A parent's blessing on her son
  Goes with this holy thing;
The love that would retain the one,
  Must to the other cling.
Remember! 'tis no idle toy:
A mother's gift! remember, boy.

DEFINITIONS.—2. Plĕdġe, *proof, evidence*. 3. In'çĕnse, *some-thing offered in honor of anyone*. Fāith, *belief* 4. Seŏff'er, *one who laughs at what is good.*

Made in United States
North Haven, CT
20 February 2025

66110889R00155